P9-DCE-450

Women Who May Never Marry

WOMEN WHO MAY NEVER MARRY

❦ ❧

The Reasons, Realities and Opportunities

by
Leanna Wolfe

Longstreet Press
ATLANTA, GEORGIA

Published by LONGSTREET PRESS, INC.
A subsidiary of Cox Newspapers,
A division of Cox Enterprises, Inc.
2140 Newmarket Parkway
Suite 118
Marietta, GA 30067

Copyright © 1993 by Leanna Wolfe

All rights reserved. No part of this book may be reproduced in any form by any means without prior written permission of the Publisher, excepting brief quotations used in connection with reviews, written specifically for inclusion in a magazine or newspaper.

Printed in the United States of America

1st printing 1993

Library of Congress Catalog Number 93-79669

ISBN: 1-56352-092-3

This book was printed by R.R. Donnelley & Sons, Harrisonburg, Virginia.

Book design by Laurie Shock.
Jacket design by Graham & Company.

TABLE OF CONTENTS

∿ • ✧

DEDICATION

To my mother, Sarah Wolfe, who so values the traditional nuclear family that a deep rebellion welled inside me, triggering the development of the ideas in this book. . . . And then, out of great love and perhaps wisdom, listened hard, invited all of her friends to hear my talk at the Palo Alto Jewish Community Center, and then admitted that my ideas do make sense, stopped bugging me about getting married and *noodged* me to stop distracting myself and to finish the book!

To my father, Irwin Wolfe, who has been a great adventurer and storyteller in his own right and knows how to find humor in just about everything. His firm sense of what's moral, right, and a good idea gave me something to rebel against. . . . Otherwise, I might never have been motivated to become an anthropologist and write such a book!

To Glen Gersmehl, who taught me much about passion for ideas, projects and people, and who made up great jokes along the way and let all of my emotions be right. If we hadn't repeatedly been unable to decide to get married, I might never have dreamed up these ideas and then believed them so deeply that I'd devote years to writing a book about them!

To Boyd Willat, who was thoroughly married by the time we met, but nonetheless became a central figure in my community and my life. He believed in me, inspired me to take my work very seriously, made me feel special, called at some very odd hours to discuss everything from my dark dramatic dreams to each newfangled theory I concocted to explain the culture's (if not my own personal) dilemmas, and most important, never ever let me feel abandoned or unloved.

To Don Byrd, who managed to slip into my life well after this book was over half-written. Despite my isolationist writing schedule and erratic mood swings, we managed to fall in love with each other. He engaged my theories, offered me stories to support them, proofread rough drafts, and made me feel precious and very loved. The intimacy we created together gave me some ever-so-valuable distance on being "me-focussed" vs. "we-focussed."

Thanks

To all the women and men who shared their stories, who went along with all of my probing for more, and willingly kept sharing.

To my last four years of anthropology students, who weathered my lectures on singles culture and the future of family, enthusiastically shared their own stories, and willingly purchased class readers stuffed with articles I wrote. When some of them assured me that this was something they'd want to read it even if they weren't trying for an "A," I knew I was on the right track.

To Cliff Carle, who painstakingly edited my book proposal, made hilarious jokes about my often less-then-lucid presentation, and designed a special set of tennis rules so that our games would be evenly matched.

To Cathy Carpenter, who back in Berkeley in 1974 became my soul sister in rebelling against every conformist act that crossed our paths, and has remained an unflinching supporter of every creative and outrageous thing I decide to do.

To Marci Mearns, who has shown me what it means to really be there for another person. Marci enthusiastically reads every treatise (and yet-to-be treatise) I manage to generate, asks for more and then stays up late with me to bitch, moan, cry, shiver and shake over how things just aren't yet the way we want them to be.

To Judith Rubenstein, with whom I've been exchanging detailed letters about sex, love, our careers, money and social theories since 1982, when I left New York City and we were both too broke to afford more than postage stamps to stay in touch. When I write to Judith everything flows—her existence as an ever-open recipient of my ideas, musings, and adventures has made me a more confident person and a better writer.

To Warren Jason, a key player in my extended family of choice. His levels of service include: scheming about the most marketable title for this book, futzing with my computer even after proclaiming I should go hire a professional, clipping articles, proofreading drafts, evaluating cover designs, being the best gossip and storyteller in town, feeding me the most exquisite meals and throwing some of the best parties I've ever attended.

To my sister, Roselyn Mena, her husband, Jesús, nephew Francisco and niece Sonia, who have a marvelous ability to make and hold onto friends. To me, they are a living model of a fully social and community-minded nuclear family.

To all the singles groups who invited me and *paid* me to speak to their members. Their heated discussions and enthusiastic receptions assured me that if I could ever isolate myself enough to write this book, lots of people would buy it!

To the people of Mani, Yucatan, Mexico who in January 1976 invited me into their village. Being included in their traditional extended family for the last seventeen years has provided me a warm loving model for what else is humanly possible.

To Carol Stieglitz, whose enthusiasm for my about-to-be-discarded book proposal caused me to send it out to another round of publishers. Her resonance with my ideas and delight in commenting on my drafts made me feel purposeful and important.

To Joyce Schwarz, who, despite her own book deadline, was always chock full of suggestions, referrals, stories, and poignant insights.

To Annie Siegel, who, beyond being a caring friend, so responded to what I was writing that she'd feed me her personal adventures, sometimes on a daily basis, knowing full well that they could all end up in the pages you are about to read!

To Jai Josefs, who could find an argument with just about every point made in this book, but nonetheless hangs in as a supportive friend and artist.

To Warren Farrell, who showed me it's possible to be a successful author and a thoroughly original private person. His love and friendship inspired me to be an author in my own right.

To Douglas Frohman, who explained the dynamics of procrastination in such a way that I stopped doing it and found more pleasure (and relief) in writing this book.

To Dawn Moore and Lynn Jennings, my roommates when most of this was being generated and nobody much was listening. They listened and shared and I appreciate it.

To my agent, Mike Hamilburg, who listened and cared. He guided me through writing my proposal and offered me rock-solid encouragement.

To Ron Reagan and Jane Whitney, who featured me as a guest on their talk shows before I had a deal for this book. Their enthusiasm for my ideas helped me believe even more in myself and moreover, helped my publisher believe in me, too.

To John Yow at Longstreet Press, who was enthusiastic from the moment my query letter landed on his desk. He kept me in good spirits despite all the calamities that might have kept me from finishing the book. He and everyone at Longstreet made me feel that what I was up to was absolutely worth it.

To Poppy, my cat, who knows when to be present and when to be absent . . . who somehow has geared herself to my erratic life rhythms and is an excellent judge of who should stay over and who should leave.

And countless other friends, family, and supporters for whom it would fill another volume explaining what they've done and what I like about them. They include: Phyllis Wexler, Gayle Kirschenbaum, Sherry Stern, Cynthia Smith, Madeline Press, Lois Arkin, Deborah Borys, Dennis Bernstein, Larry Becker, Barry Benioff, John Webb, Diane Nelson, Orrin Charm, Caren Finnerman, David Chornow, Scott Kaye, Michelle November, Joel and Marion Moskowitz, Bob and Janet Wolfe, Alan and Cindy Garner, Chris Boehm, Woody Clark, Tom Belmonte, Rayna Rapp, Phil Kilbride, Caitlin Mullin, Sharon Wright, Sandy Orellana, Judith Boyd, Bob Ducibella, Robert Linden, Harry Deligter, Eric Ehlenberger, Ned Einstein, Celia and Ed Freiberg, Gary Geller, Jerry Gillies, Carolyn Karr, Peter Glassberg, Tom Glover, Liz Hargrove, Maggie Haney, Luis Torres, Mark Haefele, Jeff Hirsch, Terry Hopwood, Lisa Hecht, Alida Nauman, Claire and Chuck Thurston, Felice Willat, Michele Weitzman, Patricia Stewart, Patti Taylor, Lucy Ramirez, Shirley Van Edgon, Jim Burry, Steve Konigsberg, Carol Hemingway, Mark Maier, Alexander Lehr, Dennis Lofgren, Jackie and Dan Stewart, Akasa Levi, Rina Malinger, Ken Marton, Marie Ary, Terrence McNally, Karen Merchant, Lloyd Miller, Larry Mantle, Irene Neuman, Lisa Onodera, Philip Rodriguez, Arhata, Michael Perry, Eric and Martina Peterson, Neville Raymond, Sarah Spurr, Mair Simone, Kent Strumpell, Allison Trinkl, Barbara Trent, Ellen Sakoloff, Valri Swift, Lynda Smith, Nicholas Rogers, Ellen Schmalholts, Beverly Trainer, Rae Newman, Jeff Cazanov, Henrietta Finnegan, Janet Aniline, Sierra Byrd, Robert and Becky Martin, Judy Montell, Jim Sandiford, Bill Myers, Deborah Anapol, and the late Wayne Satz. And the following groups: the Society for the Scientific Study of Sex Writers Group, Gemini Manor Sunday Salons, Los Angeles Sex Education Resources, Robert Ross' Soup Night, Live the Dream, The Spark Group, The Business Edge, The Peace and Justice Resource Center of Seattle, The Circle of Power, and the Thursday Night Let Go.

A Personal Introduction

Just about every woman who writes a book telling other women how to manage their personal lives in some way displays herself as a shining example of that "right life."

If she's writing a book on how to get married, she may proudly present herself as a once lonely single woman who is now happily wed, thanks to her method.

A woman who tells other women how to take charge of career and money matters may proclaim herself to be enjoying the fruits of her financial success. Newly slender creatures who have conquered food addiction may offer themselves as proof of their theories in their books on food and dieting.

And the woman whose book teaches other women how to rejuvenate the traditionally feminine parts of their personas may play alluring and demure in public, leaving many to wonder how many hours a day she can keep up that front.

So what does the woman who just wrote *Women Who May Never Marry* have to say for herself? Is she a confirmed spinster? Does she have a horrible personality, a homely appearance, or a complete lack of social skills? Truthfully, I suffer from none of the above. Moreover, it's certainly possible that someday I'll marry.

Seven years ago, at the "advanced" age of thirty-three, I left the San Francisco area and a seven-year-long relationship to further a television writing and producing career in Los Angeles. For the first time in my life, I was truly single, and L.A.'s singles scene intrigued the social anthropologist in me. In that first year, I experimented with everything: personal ads, singles dances, matchmaking services, private clubs, you name it. Part of me wanted to check it all out and explore the singles scene. Another part of me was still in painful shock from the realization that the man I had planned to marry and raise a family with was not going to be my husband. It took me the next four years to separate emotionally from him and to realize that I could not only live on my own, but enjoy it immensely.

My first year of singleness was coupled with a real desperation to replace the lost man in my life with "husband material." I figured since I had already felt so ready to marry, all I needed to do was replace the potential bridegroom. But I ended up not doing that—because I discovered it was fun to have lots of men in my life. Because I found I needed to be myself on my own—to run out of money, to accumulate little windfalls, to buy what I wanted to buy or buy nothing at all, to eat whenever and whatever I wished, to fall asleep on the living room couch or stay up all night. And because I realized I didn't want to be accountable to any one man.

Next, I realized that one reason I stayed single was because single people were becoming a breaking-edge social phenomenon, and I wanted to be a part of it. Seventy-seven million Americans adults, or forty-one percent of the U.S. population, are now single, up from thirty-two percent in the early '60s. These figures raise hard questions about the direction of the family and the future of intimacy.

I realized that the anthropologist in me had been immersed in a study of the singles culture and had a lot to say. But when I committed myself to writing this book, I suddenly felt all of the pain of being single. I was no longer the perky social anthropologist who could tell readers why there are so many single people and what the future of the family might be. And I was also a little too alone. In fact, if I felt so alone that when there was no one I could even spin a fantasy relationship about, I couldn't get myself to write at all. Despite my conviction that women don't need to be married (or even coupled) to be happy, I was miserable when there wasn't some guy I was growing closer to or at least could fantasize about growing closer to. I felt horribly fraudulent. Then I remembered our human history of social interdependence, and thanked my emotions for not steering anyone (especially me) down a path of total emotional, spiritual, social, and sexual independence.

The primary research method that social anthropolgists use is participant-observation. To do this we both involve ourselves in the cultures we study as well as step back and reflect upon that culture as an outsider. While I discuss quantitative findings (like the results of Census Bureau studies), the examples I offer are drawn from interviews as well as participant-observation. Real women's (and men's) life stories are far more intricate, varied, and multidimensional than the brief archtypal examples I discuss. When I refer to someone as a "pain-averter" or a "magic lady," by no means am I implying that's all who they are. While the names I've given my characters are fictional, their stories, challenges, and dilemmas are based on real people.

The thinking behind this book differs from many of the other "how to bring true love, marriage and happiness into your life" books. First of all, I'm not a psychotherapist, psychiatrist, or a social worker, and so my data base was not confined to a set of clients in pain about their lack of love and intimacy, who fear they may never marry. I had and have no interest in conducting a study to determine the psychological factors contributing to singleness. Being a social anthropologist, I looked at normal rather than deviant behavior. I looked at the vast numbers of ordinary, non-psychotic women who understand that not marrying is not the end of the world. In fact, the more I publicized my research interests, the more women I met who freely acknowledged their lack of interest in marriage. As far as they were concerned, a good life full of intimacy and community is possible for singles.

Women Who May Never Marry is for people who believe they are healthy. In it I discuss what's right with women's social and sexual behavior. I reveal the smart logical reasons why women feel, live, and react as they do. In some ways, this book is simply an affirmation of the obvious. But in this age of remaking oneself in order to simply be loved, it's ideas are absolutely essential.

I believe there is more for us to gain in figuring out why we are the way we are than in trying to make ourselves into people we can never really be. Understanding our lives as they are can be much saner than chastising ourselves for not performing the impossible. What I can offer you as a reader is guidance to understanding forces larger than all of us, and to using that understanding to build peace inside yourself.

Chapter 1

THE REAL REASONS WHY MANY WOMEN MAY NEVER MARRY

•••

*T*here have always been women who never married. But because marriage was seen as crucial for a proper woman's social identity and economic survival, these women were disparaged as spinsters, old maids and mistresses. Today, however, record numbers of physically attractive and financially independent single women don't need to trade sex and/or homemaking services for economic support. Their mere existence challenges traditional male/female dynamics and the functions of marriage. For many women, getting married no longer marks the transition into adulthood. In fact, a woman who lives on her own may achieve a more enduring social and financial independence than one who goes from her parents' home directly into marriage. You may be one of the women who have concluded that marriage may actually be an obstacle, rather than a goal, along your path toward personal fulfillment.

If you are single, you are not alone. In fact, nearly forty-two percent of our adult population (defined by the Census as anyone over fifteen) is single. In contrast, just thirty years ago, only thirty-two percent of the adult population was single. A dramatic change in public opinion is linked to this demographic shift. In 1960, single people were pitied. Now it is considered acceptable, if not desirable, to be single. Today, some of the most highly accomplished, beautiful, well-educated, and intelligent women do not happen to be married.

These days, married people are not necessarily happier than single people. In fact, Jessie Bernard's 1972 study, *The Future of Marriage*, showed that single females are likely to be much happier than married females. The happiest females are often divorcées who have no interest in remarrying, while the most miserable males are recently divorced and not yet remarried. Why? Many women experience marriage as servants and caretakers to husbands and children, and divorce often opens up a whole new world of freedom. Meanwhile, since most men don't develop ways to share emotionally or spiritually outside of a primary romantic relationship as easily as women do, marriage remains the only arena many of them have for gaining the intimacy all humans need.

Perhaps the most startling statistic today is the record number of adults now living alone. One hundred years ago, single or studio apartments were unheard of—everyone, married or not, lived in family-sized dwellings. Few societies have the technology and support services that make it possible to live alone. The Turkana, a tribe in Kenya, do not even consider single life feasible. When a woman becomes widowed, she marries into another household and becomes a second or third wife. Since the Turkana don't have fast foods, microwave ovens, maids, laundries, or child-care services, their homemaking responsibilities require at least two women to maintain most households.

In addition to the startling leap in singles, studies also show there are more of us living on our own. Twenty-three percent of the U.S. population now lives alone. In the city of Los Angeles, thirty-one percent of adults live alone. So more of us are spending more time by ourselves. We're probably not getting greeted, hugged, kissed, and attended to as frequently as humans previously have been, nor as frequently as our non-human primate cousins consider normal.

As an anthropologist, I've had the opportunity to study primate social behavior. In their natural habitats, nearly every primate species lives in groups; they spend most of every day in the close physical company of others. They may be groomed by others in the group several times a day and are always within earshot of fellow group or troop members.

We human primates also come out of a social tradition. Our hunter-gatherer ancestors lived in tribes. About 10,000 years ago, they began to domesticate plants and animals and settled into family-based villages. Even thousands of years later, when these families migrated to other parts of the world, their kin alliances remained very important, prescribing with whom members would live and how they would work. Only in very recent history have we humans lived apart from our extended families.

Few of us now work together as families or even own businesses with other family members. Just as many farm-based families faced the fact that they could not continue subdividing their holdings for generation after generation of children, the industrial revolution began to lure young men and women to work in urban factories. Rather than moving an entire multigenerational family to seek employment in far-flung cities, the smallest family unit moved. That unit was the nuclear family.

How did this migration affect our social relationships? For the first time, women were separated from their sisters, cousins and mothers. The social network among women who kept house, cooked, and raised children disappeared, as did an intricate social, emotional, and spiritual support system. Instead, many women directed all these needs to one other person—their husbands. Increased expectations and pressure to be so much to one other person led many to profound dissatisfaction with their spouses, and ultimately, to divorce.

We still come into the world as a result of a social union. For most of us, our mothers and fathers formed some kind of social, emotional, and certainly sexual relationship that caused us to be born. Despite new fertility technologies making it possible for a woman and a man to produce a baby without a social or even sexual relationship, nature's plan was for us to be born from a caring, cooperative union. It isn't necessary, however, for that union to last a lifetime. In fact, according to anthropologist Helen Fisher, the average duration of a romantic human relationship is four to seven years. In strictly biological terms, that's just the time needed for the resulting child to be weaned enough so that its mother no longer requires intense support from its father.

Our romantic and religious notions about marrying for life are rooted in a time when the average life expectancy was about forty years. Marriage existed primarily as a social means to insure biological reproduction. Then, younger women were the most desirable marital partners because they were the most fertile. Although today's women in their mid-thirties or forties are usually capable of bearing children, our cultural notions of female beauty remain rigidly linked to these antiquated notions of fertility.

WHY ARE WE SO CONCERNED OVER WOMEN WHO MAY NEVER MARRY?

When a woman chooses not to or doesn't manage to marry, it is presumed that during her entire life she will be socially, sexually, and economically independent. This can be seen as dangerous or threatening to:

1. Her parents, because they recall the spinsters and old maids of yesteryear and fear that despite their daughters best intentions, she, too, will be left lonely, poor and unloved.

2. The male establishment, because they're terrified of the larger implications of such an across-the-board social revolution, with large numbers of women requiring full-time salaries, benefits, and even retirement plans.

3. The married heterosexual members of the communities in which these women live, because the mere existence of stylish, successful single women threatens the stability of marriage.

4. "Women who fear they may never marry," whom I've dubbed the "The Female Mafia," because they are terrified of doing anything that might jeopardize their own or their best girlfriends' chances of marrying. In their fear, they maintain virtue by upholding proper dress and dating codes and imposing a rigid morality.

DEMOGRAPHICS

Contrary to popular belief, 1987 census data reveals that there are actually more unmarried men than women in every age group up until sixty-five. After sixty-five, the men who are still alive are more likely to be married. However, the numbers once told a different story. Men used to outlive women, because many women died in childbirth. Improved birth management and wider availability of birth control, along with the unequal pressures on men's lives, produced what is now a four-to-one survival rate of women to men over the age of sixty. Men are much more likely to die in war, homicides, urban gang activities, job-related accidents, and from the stress-related dangers like heart attacks and alcoholism that are linked to being permanent full-time providers for women and children.

Consequently, today's single women in their thirties and forties who would like to marry a man slightly older than themselves are finding that the pickings are getting pretty slim. This marriage squeeze is also a result of the post–World War II baby boom (1946–1959). Broad-scale wartime service explains why there were not enough births in the early 1940s to provide appropriately aged males who could marry the swell of females born in the mid-1940s and early '50s. Now, as baby-boom men reach their late thirties and forties, their preferences often dip down to women seven to ten years their junior. As these men court and marry women in their twenties and early thirties, they leave today's woman in her late thirties and forties who desires a man in his forties potentially squeezed out of marriage.

Professional African-American women who desire to marry similarly aged, successful, and educated African-American men are experiencing perhaps the most dramatic marriage squeeze. At present, single white women are twice as likely to marry as single black women. One reason is that black men marry interracially at four times the rate of black women. Black women are the least likely of any U.S. ethnic group to intermarry. Other factors reducing the numbers of marriageable black men include war, disease, and homicide. While African-Americans make up just seven percent of the U.S. population, black men comprise twenty-three percent of the AIDS victims, forty-five percent of the prison population, and eighteen percent of the active military. As a result, black women have raised families on their own at a much higher rate than any other U.S. ethnic group. As reported on ABC's "20/20," while about nine percent of all U.S. households are single-parent families, sixty percent of all black households are headed by single women. By the year 2000, this figure is projected to be at least seventy percent.

Concern over a marriage squeeze came to a head in 1986 when a Harvard-Yale study boldly predicted that only five percent of single, college-educated women over thirty-five and one percent of such women once they reached forty would ever tie the knot. While the study's conclusions have since been challenged and revised, demonstrating that women over thirty-five have between a thirty-two and forty-one percent probability of marrying, women at forty face the not-so-ponderous odds of seventeen to twenty-three percent. That's twenty-three times higher than the one percent prediction the mainstream media gleefully broadcast when they pandered to the "Will I be single forever?" anxieties of over-thirty women. (For the story behind the censorship and manipulation of these figures see Susan Faludi's *BACKLASH: The Undeclared War Against American Women*).

Perhaps the Harvard-Yale study's designers were addressing an irrelevant concern. They presumed that women who had focused on their careers in their twenties and thirties would all have a change of heart by their mid-thirties and want to settle into a traditional marriage. Their concern might be analogous to a study of the eating habits of self-made vegetarians, which demonstrated that only five percent have the likelihood of ever again eating meat. These vegetarians didn't change their eating habits with the secret hope of someday changing back; likewise, many single women may not want to remarry, making the Harvard-Yale study inherently pointless.

What the Harvard-Yale study ought to have considered were the social, economic, and political factors that had made marriage uninteresting to women who came of age in the 1960s and 1970s. They might instead have focused on what these women had done rather than on what they had never set out to do. In writing this book, my first questions were, "Why are single women single?" and "Who will they become?" rather than "What's wrong with single women?" or "Will these women ever marry?"

FEMINISM

As baby-boom women reached adulthood, they witnessed the demystification of the "feminine mystique." They saw those picture-perfect Ozzie-and-Harriet marriages of the '50s swept away by a huge wave of divorces by the mid-'70s. Their mothers, who initially appeared content with laundering the white shirts worn with their husbands' gray flannel suits and preparing lemonade for their daughters' Brownie meetings, suddenly looked hard in the mirror and didn't like what they saw. Proclaiming that a life engineered for the service of others was just not enough, they sought ways to express themselves as complete human beings.

Feminism, fueled by an agenda for political and economic equity, implored women to focus on their careers and themselves. Young women felt empowered to believe they could be anything they wanted to be. Under these conditions, fewer young women chose to marry, or at least chose to marry in the ways their 1950s mothers had.

Feminism also intensified the battle of the sexes. As women made their own money and opened their own doors, their expectations for good communication with men increased. They basked in the sisterhood of consciousness-raising groups and admonished men for their lack of adeptness in emotional expression.

While male/female communication may have actually increased in the post-1960s era, the criteria for partner satisfaction increased even more. In earlier times, men and women did not expect as much from each other; women's deepest intimacies were shared with other women, and men's with other men. Marriages were much more socio-economic arrangements than realms for complete emotional and spiritual fulfillment. The '60s and '70s changed all that, and the divorce rate has hovered at fifty percent ever since.

Feminism gave women much greater permission to openly explore and express their sexuality. Consciousness-raising groups gave their members a place to discuss and explore their sexual desires and orgasmic potential. As women began to perceive themselves as independent, they began to take their sexual satisfaction seriously. Sex was no longer something a wife did for her husband to keep him happy; instead, it became something that women developed preferences for, and they became articulate enough about them to ask for what they wanted. Some young women today forthrightly demand sexual performance of their boyfriends. The authors of *Remaking Love* contend that the sexual revolution of the '60s and '70s might more accurately be seen as "women's sexual revolution" because men continued to do what they always did sexually, but for the first time women were freed from labels like "virgin" or "whore"; they could freely be sexual in or out of marriage.

The decision to question the necessity and worth of marriage didn't occur just to young women in the '60s and '70s. College and career women today contend that feminism has given them, too, license to pursue independent dreams. When I speak as a guest lecturer on college campuses today, many of the young women in my audiences want me to tell them how to fashion a life as a single and fulfilled woman. They doubt that traditional marriage is a viable answer for their future. When they find out that I am single, they are envious, and want to figure out how to do it, too. The thought of finding a man who will save, protect, and provide for them holds very little interest.

Finally, feminism gave lesbians permission to openly express their sexuality. Rather than hiding in marriages of convenience, lesbians could now explore their deeper potentials as lovers, partners, and as women. They are certainly among the women who no longer have any reason to consider heterosexual marriage.

The Singles Business

The singles business had boomed by the '80s, realizing enormous profits from the dubious unification of highly self-centered potential "Mr. and Ms. Rights." By the time single baby-boom women were ready to have babies, many felt that "all the good men" were gone. For them, a "good man" was confident, powerful, physically fit and financially successful, as well as warm, sexy, emotionally expressive, attentive, and supportive of his partner's career. These were enormous requirements, and there have never been large numbers of men who could qualify.

Many of the single people I interviewed have extensive wish lists for their prospective partners. Chuck, thirty-three, has covered nearly half the wall space in his bedroom with his list and the various personal ads he's placed. His requirements specify in minute detail what his dream woman should look like — her proportions, build, and ethnicity, as well as her food preferences and spiritual inclinations. Chuck even goes so far as to insist that his Ms. Right should be interested in being an assistant and eventually a collaborator in his business.

People like Chuck ask for so much because they are used to getting what they want. With their "quick-fix" consciousnesses, they expect fast, permanent answers. And in our intensely consumerist culture, they have come to expect that the ease with which one can purchase material things ought to translate into a similar ease in acquiring love.

Another reason people like Chuck ask for so much is that they simply have *inflated expectations*. Many of them have come to believe that they ought to be able to find an absolutely perfect partner, perhaps a soul mate. In our lives we've seen technology deliver stupendous advances; plus our culture very much enforces intense romantic fantasies. Men, beginning in adolescence, gaze long and hard at air-brushed, surgically altered *Playboy* centerfold models and fantasize that their woman will look at least as good. Meanwhile, today's women, as young girls, were the first generation to receive not just baby dolls, but adult Barbie and Ken dolls, which enabled them to spin (and sometimes believe) endless home, hearth, and romance stories.

These inflated expectations have created an across-the-board revision of what we want our partners to be. As women become economically independent, their expectations for the men in their lives changes. Women today don't expect men to be the sole provider of social identity and finances, but to be adept at expressing their feelings. Men, meanwhile, feel threatened by such demands.

In the past, satisfying a woman was a straightforward task. She could be bought gifts and taken out to dinner; once married, a man's labor could finance home and family life. In trade for being a financial provider, men received intimacy from a wife and family who loved him, as well as a full spectrum of homemaking services and a receptive, if not willing, lover. Now our inflated expectations, coupled with a deflated marketplace, have wreaked havoc on our relationships. Many men expect women to be their financial partners, while career women come home with emotional sharing expectations that men remain unable to satisfy.

What do men really want from women? Probably something analogous to what Kevin Costner's character in *Field of Dreams* got: a woman who totally believes in and supports her man's dream, however preposterous or unlikely. This wife so stands by her husband's fantasy that a legendary baseball team suddenly appears on the ball diamond she's supported him to build. The final payoff? Together, they share the same emotional moment, rejoicing in the arrival of the fruits of *his* fantasy.

But in real life, though most independent professional women will encourage their partners' success, few will drop everything to be their husband's chief assistant/cheerleader. In fact, the only woman I've met recently who is doing her all for a man is Sophie, a seventy-four-year-old grandmother who works nights and weekends in her son's law offices. However, she admits that beyond a sincere desire to help him succeed, in large part her motive is to get time away from her recently retired husband, who lounges around the house all day!

FEAR OF INTIMACY

Another factor affecting many singles' inability to sustain a relationship is the fear of intimacy. Of course, sexually transmitted diseases like AIDS and herpes can fuel such fears. And the statistics are frightening: To date, 253,448 people in the U.S. have been diagnosed with AIDS, and 171,890 have died. As of March 1993, the Centers for Disease Control estimated that 1.5 million of U.S. residents are now HIV infected.

Though you can fight fears of physical intimacy by practicing safer sex, it can be harder to confront fears of emotional intimacy. Hurtful past adult relationships or mistreatment during childhood can result in such fears; many of us are also afraid of being abandoned, overly controlled, smothered, or losing ourselves in a relationship.

One way to understand our fear of intimacy is to look at how we were raised and how that affects us as adults. I call the programming we were given as children for how to negotiate the world an *emotional map*. For example, Susan, thirty-two, was raised in a working-class family and given a particular set of strategies for survival, which included hoarding things she thought she might need some day, and being a careful shopper. She developed the sense that she didn't deserve the good things in life—these, she came to believe, were for people with greater financial means than herself and her family.

As an adult professional, Susan still operates with the emotional map of her childhood. (See Chapter Nine for more information on how to repair a faulty emotional map.) She appears to spend the income she earns, but emotionally she still lives as if she doesn't deserve unconditional love. This fear of intimacy has led her to feel comfortable only with unavailable men (e.g., those who are married, live out of town, or are otherwise occupied). In such relationships, she safely avoids anything "too good" or "too loving."

She openly admits that her continual interest in unavailable men allows her a drama so absorbing that she barely has time or attention to focus on her career or community. She devotes an inordinate amount of time dreaming and scheming about how to get attention and time from a seemingly endless array of not very available men. Whenever she manages to actually see one of them, she then spends days processing the experience by writing letters, poems, and entries in her journal as well as by talking about every detail with friends. For now, this activity is more interesting to her than getting married, and certainly satisfies her baseline social and emotional needs.

WHY SOME SINGLES ARE NOT LOOKING

Many single people choose not to look for a special partner. Their lives may feel complete just as they are—loneliness may tug inside, but open looking would jinx their chances. They believe people who look too hard must be overly desperate, single-minded, and boring.

In cities, one of the major reasons people don't look is that they're "married to their work." Women, as well as men, may decide the payoffs are greater and more enduring if they direct their energies into their careers rather than into relationships. Working single mothers perhaps have the least time to devote to meeting a partner. Every moment they're not on the job, it's likely they're attending to the needs of their children.

Single people beyond their mid-thirties who live in small towns might be considered "geographic isolates." While doing research for this book, I met several single people in their late thirties and forties who lived in small Mississippi towns. They readily agreed that they already knew of or had dated everyone of marriageable age and status in their towns. Jackson, forty-four, recalls that the last woman he dated came to town several years ago on business. While he says he wouldn't mind meeting more women, he also admits that he's grown comfortable with the lack of pressure (due to the lack of possibilities) to change his single status.

Sandy, thirty-eight, who lives in a Mississippi town less than two hours from New Orleans, has made peace with being single. Like Jackson, she, too, knows everyone in town. Occasionally a man will split from his partner, expanding her pool of possibilities from zero to one! While she freely admits she could move to New Orleans (where her pool of possible partners would expand many-fold), she'd rather stay where she is, where everyone in town knows her, where her family is nearby to help when she needs them, and where she can listen to crickets and fifteen kinds of birds every evening by her riverside bungalow.

Other ways single women can isolate themselves from the challenges and heartaches of dating is to become "physical appearance isolates." They remain overweight despite knowing they'd receive much more male attention if they were to lose weight. These women's excess weight functions as a safeguard from being treated as a sex object rather than a full person. They don't have to be wary of men's ulterior motives, unlike many attractive professional women who develop laser-like stategies to sort out professional from personal invitations.

Male deception accounts for another reason some women have stopped looking. A man may don financial "make-up" just as easily as women apply lipstick, eyeliner, and mascara. Gloria, thirty-five, was taken for a lot more than a date when she innocently believed a shy Texan who told her that he was Randy Meisner of The Eagles. He invited her out to lunch, told her stories of a lavish life in France and on the Malibu coast, promised gifts, surprises, and a trip to tour Europe with his current group, Poco. He gave her several weeks to fantasize about what life with him could be like. Once he sensed she was hooked and her confidence in him was high, he called her long distance and asked her to wire him money, claiming that he needed cash to purchase a discount airline ticket for her flight to Europe. It wasn't until she contacted the real Randy Meisner's management company that she realized she had been talking to an imposter. Even in this extreme example, Gloria voices what a lot of women feel after being led along a primrose path, confiding, "Some not very feminist/independent part of me still wanted to believe the imposter—I really wanted someone to dramatically step in and give me the good life!"

The more disappointments—financial or social—women find in men, the more women decide to make it on their own. Many single mothers have put remarriage on the back burner, while growing numbers of successful single women are finding ways to become mothers on their own. (See Chapter Four, "Bio-Time-Clock Women," for more information on this subject.)

Many single people are just not interested in getting married. These include divorced women uninterested in returning to the role of caretaker to another man and more children (see Chapter Seven for more on women who may never remarry), and African-American women who have made peace with their lives despite the shallow pool of marriageable African-American men.

Women in small southern towns are more likely to be part of an intact extended family. Their families relieve them of the monthly financial pressures experienced by many urban working women as well as provide child-care assistance, food, emotional support, and, at times, shelter. When Viola, thirty-six, divorced, she left Detroit and returned to her extended family in Mississippi. Despite the lower salary she'd be earning as a secretary, she knew that by going back to Mississippi she could depend on her mother to babysit. If her salary didn't stretch through the end of the month, her mother would certainly invite her over for dinner and for the holidays; there would always be family to come home to.

Some single women and men simply enjoy the excitement of meeting and dating an endless array of new people. They may like the freedom of not having to be accountable to anyone else and being able to keep their own hours and live their own lives. Others have built (or are in the process of building) functional social networks that fill many of the family-type needs traditionally met through marriage. (Building such a network, an "extended family of choice," is discussed in Chapter Ten.)

WHAT'S REALLY GOING ON?

Our society has become intensely segmented. We've become accustomed to having multiple sources to fill our social, emotional, and financial needs. Moreover, it's become apparent that no one person can be or become everything. Yet, more than ever, this intense segmentation makes us try even harder to find that one person who really understands, who can help us feel connected both to him or her and to the universe. We simultaneously fear intimacy and crave attention. We want to be loved like babies, as well as to have the space to think our own thoughts and make our own messes.

Some of this need for space has to do with the American tradition of individualism. While many world cultures foster group action and sensitivity to the needs and feelings of group members, our culture doesn't. We are products of the westward expansion and rugged individualism. Our cultural ideal is to make it on our own—to survive against all odds. While Japanese cultural heroes might commit *harikari* to redeem themselves from having wronged someone else, our cultural ideal is to engage the services of the most cunning attorney who skillfully weasels us out of the crime.

Many of us also want space because we've felt controlled. We don't want anyone ever again to get under our skin and tell us what to do. One of the benefits of leaving the family farms and moving to cities was being able to break away from the influence of the extended family. Individuals who came to cities lived their own lives; they were free to be whoever they wanted to be. They no longer had to fit into family patterns or meet family expectations.

How does family life trap us? Often, people who feel trapped in every other area of their lives resort to romantic or family relationships to act powerful. The powerlessness they feel in public can inversely affect how controlling they will be in private. Those of us who have been the brunt of this "reactive power" may so hate it that we'll do everything we can consciously (and subconsciously) to keep away from controllers. Thus, we feel free and safe when no one is getting under our skin, trying to read our moods, telling us how they want us to live or spend our futures.

Some women like Linda, thirty-eight, find themselves obsessing over unavailable men as a way to subconsciously avoid being controlled. Two years ago at a professional conference she met Scott, forty-three, who lives in a distant city. During the conference, they spent nearly every waking hour together, enjoying much more intimacy than either usually tolerated in their hometowns. After the conference Scott reached a fantasy level of perfection to Linda. While the real Scott was easily as quirky and difficult as all the other men she'd known in her life, the fantasy Scott quickly became a passionate obsession. Despite seeing him only a couple of times, she feels safe expressing passionate love to him because of the distance (both geographic and in time) between them.

Some of the more iconoclastic among us are single as an expression of rebellion against the conformity imposed by the media—by commercials, fashion, everything that makes us feel that there's only one thing to like and one way to be. We choose almost purposely not to like anything that we're told to like.

A final dilemma we face is the incongruity between our cultural and religious belief in marriage "for life" and the reality of life in the late 20th century. Many of us will have between four and seven careers during our lifetimes. This multidimensional quality alone dramatically reduces the likelihood that anyone can truly be a lifetime match. We are then left living a painful dichotomy: Emotionally, we want what economic and social forces are keeping us from achieving. We want to be loved forever, just like Ozzie loved Harriet. However, in reality, it's increasingly less likely that we'll marry for life. Many of us spend more of our adult years between relationships, perhaps concluding that we may never marry or never remarry.

In conclusion, for most of us, the primary reasons we may not marry or remarry are directly linked to social, demographic, and economic changes. These changes have allowed us much more individual freedom to act and live independently of our families. In tandem with this freedom often comes an alienation that so mires us in the pain of being alone that we attempt to quick-fix the emptiness rather than carefully examine the causes. For most of us, these causes have an energy and impact much larger than our personal, interpersonal, and family dramas. In the next chapter, we'll examine the pressures in other times and in other cultures that have caused women not to marry, as well as how these women achieved social, emotional and community happiness.

Chapter 2

SPINSTERS, OLD MAIDS, AND FALLEN WOMEN

•••

There have always been women who did not marry. In different settings and cultures, the desirability of marriage has varied tremendously. So certainly now is not the first time in human history that a large sector of women may never marry. Looking at what happened in other times and places can provide us assurance in the form of worthy models, if not viable solutions. We'll survey women of the Second, Third, and Fourth Worlds who have not married, explore the culture and outlook of America's 19th-century spinsters, old maids, and mistresses, as well as consider reports from the front — American women now in their seventies and eighties who are proudly single by choice.

MY PERSONAL JOURNEY AND YUCATEC MAYAN WOMEN WHO MAY NEVER MARRY

I was born close to the middle of the 1950s baby boom and was raised in a suburban nuclear family in a community made up nearly entirely of families like my own. When I was very young, I was not aware of unmarried adult women. As a little girl who played elaborate games with dolls, I never imagined for a moment that I might never marry. If economics, social expectations, and educational opportunities hadn't changed dramatically over the next twenty years, it's likely I would have married and attempted to create a family much like the one I was raised in.

The first time I experienced living in another kind of family was while doing anthropological field work in Mani, a Mayan village situated near the center of Mexico's Yucatan Peninsula. When I first arrived in the mid-'70s, I witnessed and participated in the day-to-day workings of a true extended family. Everyone carried on day-to-day/face-to-face relationships with their mothers, fathers, brothers, sisters, cousins, and grandparents. This constant exposure to extended family seemed reminiscent of what my grandparents' lives might have been like before migrating to the United States from Russia and Rumania in the early 1900s. It was a world I had personally never known.

While my parents grew up in quite functional extended families in New York City, they raised my sister and me unfettered by relatives in Palo Alto, a California suburb. The four of us were the only people I considered "family." While I became aware of and eventually met grandparents, aunts, uncles, and cousins, I always sensed they were extraneous. If I wanted to be close to them, I could, but I felt no family obligation to anyone but my parents and sister.

Mani was a whole other story. From the moment I strung up my hammock in my host family's house, I belonged. My needs were noticed, and I quickly came to notice theirs and everyone attached to them. Each child who grew up in the Mani of the 1970s freely roamed between five or six houses. On a daily basis, children interacted with cousins, aunts, uncles, and grandparents. They could sleep, eat, and be lovingly cared for wherever they landed. Accepted as a family member, I, too, was fed and cared for in all the homes of my Mayan extended family.

Life in Mani has changed dramatically over the last fifteen years. Initially, only two households had clunky black-and-white television sets; now even the Mayans in the most remote outposts watch internationally produced shows on their color TVs. Before the '70s, it was unusual for anyone to complete more than an elementary-school education, but now many of the children I met eighteen years ago have degrees from universities and professional schools. These children, now adults, face a huge dilemma: Should they leave Mani to be urban professionals and abandon the extended families of their childhood, or should they abandon the profession they studied to live in a community where they are fully-known and fully belong?

Mani's young men, tempted by television images of what they might own, have left in large numbers. On a recent visit, I attended a dance where there seemed to be at least a three-to-one ratio of young women to young men. I questioned several of the women about what appeared to be very limited prospects for marriage. Their response was at best a shy giggle. Initially, I wondered why they were so unconcerned. For women in Los Angeles, in contrast, the difference between marrying and staying single can be huge. If a woman marries a wealthy man, she might live in a beautiful Bel Air home with housekeepers, gardeners, and a nanny as soon as a baby is born. An L.A. woman who has a baby on her own (as over forty percent are now doing) is more likely to face an uphill financial struggle.

Over the next several days, I observed why the Mayan women only giggled. I concluded that marrying or not marrying would have little consequence on the quality of their lives. Every Mani woman, married or single, did the same things. They cleaned houses, cooked, sewed, cared for children, and socialized with other women. Single women didn't live on their own–they were integral members of their extended families. If single women didn't live with their parents, then they were likely to live with a married brother or sister, as a full adult member of that household.

As full members of extended families, they didn't have the kind of intimacy gap many people in L.A. face. Their social, emotional, and economic needs would always be met. Moreover, they were important contributors in meeting these needs for other family members. Next, I asked about sex and children. My questions only produced shrugs and shy giggles. Again, I *looked* for answers.

Over the next several days I noted the ways these women physically interacted with their family members. Chatting, they carelessly intertwined their legs with those of their cousins and sisters, something most Americans would only do consciously with a lover. They freely hugged each other, walked hand-in-hand with other women, and shared unabashed eye contact for much longer than the second or two th average American can tolerate when not conversing. Where many Americans use sex is the sole vehicle for physical intimacy, the Mayans have a much wider spectrum of activities that everyone shares. With these in place, sex isn't as fetishized.

While there is plenty of joking about sex, the single Mayan women I engaged had little to say about the sex they might never have. Being a day-in/day-out caretaker-aunt fully satisfied their maternal desires. Since about ninety percent of a woman's waking hours were spent in the company of other women and children, the place a male partner/husband might fill was truly minimal. Finally, despite how media, education, and economics have challenged peasant women's marriageability not just in Mani, but throughout the world, the endurance of their extended families easily assures that their adult lives will be socially, economically, and emotionally complete.

VARIATIONS IN THE FUNCTION AND MEANING OF MARRIAGE

Marriage means different things in different cultures. Likewise, women who don't happen to be married are accorded different status depending on the value and availability of marriage. In Jamaica, for example, ninety-eight percent of the population are unmarried. Marriage exists as an expensive ritual that many people never manage to afford. Jamaicans, nonetheless, fall in love, live with their sweethearts, and raise families together. Out-of-wedlock births to Murphy Brown types may spark a values conflict in America, but in Jamaica such a concern would barely raise an eyebrow.

Women in many times and places have been reluctant to marry. !Kung girls of Africa's Kalahari desert, for example, are filled with many doubts about marriage. They may decide that the young man to whom they were betrothed is totally unattractive and resist sleeping with him. Meanwhile, they may actively sneak off with men who are more to their liking. Eventually, as many of their stories go, they find their betrothed acceptable, and settle into enduring marriages.

Much of what allows a woman the freedom to consider not marrying or to fully reject marriage is the awareness that she can survive just fine without a husband. The !Kung, as traditional hunter-gatherers, have had no private property to entice a prospective wife or to pass on to their heirs. Thus, a young woman may not feel compelled to work things out with her husband in order to better survive. In fact, according to anthropologist Marjorie Shostak, some !Kung women admit to having a lover in every neighboring band, contending that these minor alliances better meet their needs for food and sleeping spots when visiting than just having a single husband in their home band.

Over the last several centuries, marriage has drifted in and out of style, depending on economics, education, demographics, politics, and shifts in attitudes regarding what a fulfilled woman's life could be. Life's fragility during America's Colonial Period may have caused close to ninety-six percent of women to marry. After the Revolutionary War, America was a land of dreams and possibilities. Educational and career opportunities abounded for girls; by the middle of the 18th century, growing numbers of women were not marrying. Marriage became a far more deliberate act. New emotional and psychological expectations caused a traumatic transition from singleness to marriage. Some girls saw marriage as constraining and confining, inhibiting them from expressing their true selves. These fears about loss of self, or possible loss of life from the dangers of childbirth, further justified their reluctance to marry.

However, by the late 19th century, Americans by and large regarded marriage as the only natural and desirable state for an adult women. Marriage signified normalcy and health, despite the pride and success of spinsters. Social historian Ellen K. Rothman notes a young physician's observation:

> *A lot of nervous diseases and psychosis, and morbid ideas of all kinds are peculiar to unmarried women and widows. . . . How often they all disappear like a shot at marriage.*

While present-day physicians would be hard-pressed to make such claims about marriage as women's ultimate panacea, the writings of late 19th-century women defended and enjoyed the benefits of singleness, but also valued marriage. To them, only marriage completed and fulfilled a woman. While they might pretend an interest in charities, what they really wanted were husbands and children. Then, true happiness and usefulness could be theirs.

The popularity of marriage at this time was perhaps a result of changing notions of what should happen between husbands and wives. Women's temperance reformers challenged taverns and houses of prostitution. Husbands who wanted to keep their marriages were admonished against squandering their earnings on alcohol and loose women. Thus, the notion of "companionate marriage" arose. Marriage, rather than simply a union where a man traded financial support for domestic services, became regarded as a relationship in which husband and wife lived together in support of each other's emotional well-being.

Despite the changing regard for marriage, by the early 1900s the numbers of educated single Americans remained high. More than sixty percent of women in a 1914 survey who graduated from major East

Coast colleges, including Radcliffe, Barnard, and Smith, remained single. Similarly, nearly a third of men who graduated from Harvard in 1870 were still single in their forties. Since marriage was at best an infrequently chosen option by the last century's best-educated, most prolific women, let's consider what the lives of spinsters were really about.

SPINSTERS AND OLD MAIDS

At the turn of the century, single women inhabited a completely separate world from married women. Paralleling the feminist movement launched in the late 1960s, increased education and unprecedented opportunities to work outside the home raised women's expectations for fulfillment and contributed to their view of marriage as optional. "Single blessedness" was often regarded as preferable to being married to a man one did not love. Ellen Rothman cited one young schoolteacher in the late 19th century:

> How infinitely better a loving helpful life without a mate—free to think and feel and do—not cramped by a necessary unsuitable companion.

Newspapers and magazines proclaimed that it was more worthwhile to be a useful old maid than to be a married woman without children. Louisa May Alcott wrote in the September 1887 issue of *Ladies Home Journal*:

> Spinsters are a very useful, happy, independent race, never more so than now, when all progressions are open to them and honor, fame and fortune are bravely won by any gifted members of the sisterhood.

While originally a spinster was simply a woman whose occupation was to spin, eventually the word became loaded with social definition. Despite Alcott's enlightened point of view, spinsters were regarded as sexless old maids for whom marriage seemed unlikely. They pursued gender-specific careers as governesses, teachers, librarians, and dressmakers. Seen as sad, bitter, dull, and odd, they were pitied and ridiculed. No girl in her right mind would want to grow up to be a spinster and live a life of pettiness and resignation.

Nonetheless, spinsterhood wasn't just a passing fad. It was a real-life designated identity. Certain women may have openly chosen to be spinsters both for personal freedom and the intimacy shared among a community of women. It was neither proper nor particularly possible for single women of the 19th century to live on their own, so they formed households together or lived with relatives. Like the unmarried women of Mani, they were parts of caring familial relationships, assisting in raising their nieces and nephews and creating rich community and social lives for themselves. Since women in their day were presumed to have little or no sexual desire, a celibate life was not seen as much of a sacrifice.

Since spinsters weren't burdened by family responsibilities, they had the time and interest to involve themselves in charities. They were celebrated for being selfless and virtuous. Their status may have been similar to present-day nuns and missionaries whose lives focus on service to others. In the early 1800s, a growing number of unmarried women achieved leadership positions organizing religious revivals, engaging in missionary work, establishing orphanages, and editing religious publications. They also participated in anti-slavery and temperance reform movements.

Susan B. Anthony, a spinster herself, proclaimed that single women are not halves needing complements, but well-rounded characters that all women would do well to emulate. Lacking an "other" to be defined in relation to, a spinster could be her own person. She was neither inside or outside, in the center or in the margins; she just was.

Spinsters formed homosocial relationships with each other, often living together and exchanging passionate letters. These friendships may have been virtual love affairs. The intensity of confidence and connection may have far surpassed what was considered possible, let alone desirable, with men. Perhaps the spinsters' homosocial intimacy achieved what today's women aspire to in sharing emotions with men. The spinsters' separate sphere, though not openly sexual, may have resembled the affectionate physicality of the Mayan women of Mani.

Finally, spinsters, unlike married women, were respected by men both in business and public life. The law afforded spinsters many more rights and privileges than married women. Married women were unable to keep money they earned in their own names, sign contracts, own property, or enter into professional studies, while spinsters could. If she had married, Susan B. Anthony could not have rented meeting halls or organized suffrage activities. Moreover, many of the most revered women of the last century, including Anthony, Louisa May Alcott, Elizabeth Blackwell, Florence Nightingale, Frances Willard, and Clara Barton, may very well have embraced spinsterhood to realize their life visions. Perhaps the communities they built were better foundations for achieving, building, and creating than the restrictiveness of heterosexual marriage.

MISTRESSES AND FALLEN WOMEN

Sexual expression was restricted in proper Victorian marriages—women did not have sex during menstrual periods, pregnancy or lactation, and men were advised to avoid imposing their "animal desires" on genteel wives except when necessary for conception. Thus, a huge demand for "fallen women" (who apparently did not marry) was created.

Victorian prostitutes knew men better sexually than most proper wives did, but forfeited proper relationships with men. Rather than trading a lifetime of sexual access, homemaking and child-raising services for a man's financial support, they simply traded sexual access for smaller, and often surer, amounts of money.

Working-class women—whose salaries were typically half their male counterparts'—were drawn to the relatively higher earnings possible through prostitution. They serviced transient sailors and river workers, lonely single men, and married gentlemen who justified their behavior in the name of protecting women of their own class and sparing their wives the indignity of regular sexual intercourse.

The Victorians' terror of venereal diseases created a huge demand for (presumably disease-free) virgins. One myth even held that sex with a virgin could effect a cure. Very young women were sold or kidnapped into the trade and kept in virgin brothels, which were set apart from other houses and well-insulated for sound.

Despite the willingness of impoverished nursemaids and shop girls to sell themselves for such sport, there also existed a whole technology for "restoring" virginity. Professional "virgin" prostitutes might use astringents to shrink their vaginal walls and insert a small fish bladder filled with blood to produce the requisite hymen-breaking drama.

This penchant for virgins reveals much about the attitudes of Victorian men towards women and sexuality. The fact that men found pleasure in deflowering virgins who would likely scream in bloody terror implies that men weren't seeking nurturing, skill, or assurance, but rather crude, selfish domination. In this world, women were not sexual beings. No woman in her right mind liked sex. The virgin prostitutes, especially, were simply objects for men to overpower.

It was easy for girls to go over the edge and become fallen women, to leave behind the ill-paying work of seamstresses, domestic servants, and factory textile workers and fully embrace prostitution. As textiles became industrialized, spinning fell out of favor as the major job prospect for poor women in the 1800s. The remaining option, being a domestic servant, was disparaged by girls who said they'd rather sell their bodies than scrub other people's floors. The cultural emphasis on purity meant a girl who had been "ruined" (perhaps succumbing to the advances of her domestic service employer) might as well take to the streets. With the distinction between virgin and whore so huge (and so irreparable except for "professional virgins"), deflowered girls sensed they had no other choice.

And their choice was amazingly popular. Rather than suffering in Milwaukee or Manchester, many relocated to Paris and Vienna and thoroughly cultivated their charms. Vienna in its heyday sported one prostitute for every seven men.

During the gold rush days in California and Nevada, the primary occupation of women working outside of the home was prostitution. In early mining camps, prostitutes outnumbered other women by twenty-five to one. During the decade after the gold rush, an estimated twenty percent of all women in California were prostitutes. Among Chinese immigrants the numbers were even more extreme, with two-thirds of the 3,500 women counted by the 1870 census listed as prostitutes.

With so many 19th-century American and European cities jammed with brothels, dance halls, and parlor houses, prostitution was clearly a major means of survival for working-class and fallen middle-class women. With marriage reserved for the pure and the potential for "ruin" so rampant, it's no wonder a major sector of women lived clear of the marriage market. While few may have consciously decided to become prostitutes, they clearly made the best of a society polarized by purity.

Sex workers, call girls, and escorts of today, unlike their sisters of yesteryear, do marry. No longer burdened by a cultural emphasis on "purity," they nevertheless struggle to maintain a strong, clear sense of self. Even Jan, thirty-four, who made large sums as a dominatrix and "never actually had intercourse," one day realized that her inner life force was gone. Even though she wielded the whip, she was powerless. She had played into her clients' fantasies to pay her bills. What they wanted to do never got her off. In the end, she was little different from last century's virgin whores, except that she was able to keep the same clients coming back. Shelly, a call girl for the rich and famous, like Jan, initially felt that she wouldn't get hurt because she was being paid so well. At $1,000 a date for simply being sexy and willing, she quickly raised money enough for a new car, a great apartment and lots of clothes. After a year, the money, the stars, and the parties lost their dazzle when she admitted, "I had no life of my own." She, like Jan, had become engulfed in the "meeting his needs act." A profession that can snatch one's self away only works long-term for a self-loving woman whose life purpose is so deeply ingrained that what she does with her body to make money doesn't trouble her soul.

A major, though rarely realized, fantasy of many regular johns is to marry the woman who services him so well. For a woman to stay in the business and be married, she'll need an extremely understanding (or exploitive) husband. Many single women today become prostitutes because they decide that a fee for services traded is more to their liking than marriage. Moreover, they often lack the skills, desire, and inclinations for building a marriage-type relationship.

RUSSIAN WOMEN WHO HAVE NOT NEEDED TO MARRY

The severe loss of Russian men during World War II caused Soviet society to experience a dramatic gender imbalance, with a three-to-two ratio of marriageable women to available men. By the late 1970s, ninety-five percent of males between forty and fifty were married, as compared to approximately seventy-five percent of females.

The solutions Russian women employed to meet their needs for intimacy in a world without enough men to go around, as well as their strategies for becoming mothers outside of marriage, are a story worth reviewing.

Prior to and during WWII, marriage was well-respected in the Soviet Union. The 1944 Code of Family Law emphasized the importance of the marital bond and the "communist family unit." Having children out of wedlock was discouraged; no special benefits were afforded to women who did so. Women married to satisfy personal and emotional needs, to find intellectual stimulation, to improve their standard of living, to avoid loneliness, and to become mothers.

After the war, everything changed. It became difficult, if not impossible, for Soviet women to find husbands. Many of these women did manage to have families as a result of a shift in social attitudes, legal reforms, and the offer of state assistance. Sex before and outside of marriage became widely understood, if not openly accepted. A national interest in replacing lost population resulted in a ban on non-therapeutic abortion. These changes caused many unmarried women to carry their unplanned pregnancies to term. Unmarried mothers were then offered the choice of a moderate state allowance for each child they bore or the option of placing unwanted babies, free of charge, in state homes. In 1970, one in ten Soviet babies (400,000 altogether) were born to unwed mothers.

Attitudes and expectations regarding "registered" vs. "unregistered" marriages shifted. Would-be brides were not as discriminating and did not always insist on registered marriages. A woman might regard herself as married to a man who was actually the legitimate husband in another woman's "registered" marriage. By 1970, 1,345,000 women reported that they were married, while their designated "husbands" said they were not. These women, rather than being subject to public scrutiny, were openly lauded.

The Soviet press triumphantly called for a redefinition of family to encompass simply mother and child. The press ran many letters from proud unwed mothers calling for public recognition and approval of their status. Moreover, Soviet social attitudes shifted from valuing only the "communist family unit" towards placing high value on children, no matter their origin. Children were regarded as a means of attaining a rewarding life; life's greatest disappointment, rather than never marrying, was not having children.

Parallels here in the United States abound, as our press creates companion pieces to the "Fertility of American Women: June 1992" Census Bureau report, which revealed that one in four single women between eighteen and forty-four had given birth outside of marriage. Pieces such as a two-page spread in the July 22, 1993, Los Angeles *Times*, titled "Mothers Go It Alone," celebrate older women who consciously decided to have babies on their own. Changing social attitudes, declining pressures to marry just to have a baby, and increasing numbers of professional and managerial women in the work force strongly resemble the social climate in the Soviet Union twenty to forty years ago.

JAPANESE WOMEN WHO HAVE LITTLE DESIRE TO MARRY

Japanese women outdo today's American women in their ambivalence about marriage. While American women's average age for their first marriage is now twenty-three, Japanese women average in at twenty-seven. And Japanese women are very picky. They want their husbands to be intelligent, educated, generous, wealthy, and tall (an ethnic and genetic challenge!). Japanese women can afford to be demanding — their educations and professional standings mean they can wait until someone spectacular comes around, or they can delightedly call their own shots.

An intriguing phenomenon that has captured the imagination of the Japanese press is that of the independent-minded, single Japanese women with a proclivity for "gaijin" (foreign) males. Anthropologist Karen Kelsky reports that these women, referred to as "yellow cabs" because "they can be ridden any time," have turned traditional Japanese sex roles on their heads. Rather than being docile, feminine and in need of rescue, they freely take "gaijin" men as lovers. As students, tourists, and professionals visiting places such as Hawaii and Bali, Japanese women do not consider these "gaijin" men marriage material, but simply sex objects. Usually unemployed, these playboys rely on an endless stream of Japanese women to pay for food, rent, and clothing. For the women, the Western man can be the sexy, wondrous outsider. He's what her parents and her culture have warned her about. And with marriage now more a choice than a necessity, she freely indulges. (For more on how American women indulge, see Chapter Eight, "The Sex Lives of Women Who May Never Marry.")

OLDER AMERICAN WOMEN WHO ARE PROUDLY SINGLE

Barbara Levy Simon has found that never-married American women now in their seventies and eighties are filled with peppery stories of having consciously chosen a single life. These women turned down Depression-era marriage offers, secured respected employment during the war, and opted out of the post-war '50s marriage wave.

These independent-minded women were clearly a statistical minority for the mid-20th century. In their America, marriage wasn't just for the wealthy, with prostitution the recourse of the masses. Rather, marriage was widely desired by all classes. No longer subject to marriages arranged by their families or the whims of the town matchmaker, they were the first generation of Americans who were absolutely free to choose their own spouses. Their singles culture enabled them to pick among multiple offers made possible by spending weekends at country clubs and attending social dances, and parties. This freedom certainly extended to choosing not to marry at all.

Delores, a black woman in her eighties, credits her disinterest in marriage to stories her grandmother told her about being a slave. To Delores, "marriage was dangerously close to slavery." After hearing stories of how her grandmother's every freedom was compromised, she concluded that for a woman, marriage simply substitutes a husband's rule for that of a master's.

In their world, a woman had to pretty much decide between working and marrying. Some, like actress Katharine Hepburn, contended their careers were so interesting that they literally did not have time to get married. Up until the pre-war forties, many largely female occupations, including teaching and library science, required that a woman be unmarried. Once a librarian or teacher disclosed that she had married, she would be summarily fired. A woman who sincerely enjoyed her profession might be skeptical of marriage, knowing it would obliterate her social and professional identity.

These women created sturdy social networks that endured well through middle age. Since most of them worked in sex-segregated occupations like teaching, nursing, office and social work, they readily created rich social constellations with their workmates. While male co-workers could be joked with, they were typically relegated to being no more than buddies. Among female colleagues, women built enduring and supportive communities, free from unwanted sexual advances. According to Sadie, eighty-one, the rapport she shared with other women was far more satisfying than what men offered:

> I could never quite understand why I felt so good about myself with my girlfriends and so at odds with myself when I was with the men I was seeing. With the girls, I could just be me. With the men, I had to somehow be fitting into a mold of "potential wife and mother." I liked much more to be with female companions who took me as I was than to be with men who were sizing me up as potential.

For Florence, eighty-six, the game-playing associated with courtship was so revolting that she, too, chose her girlfriends over marriage:

> The things my girlfriends did to get a man didn't interest me. Some even

alarmed me. Can you imagine a capable girl "playing dumb" with her beau or faking helplessness? At about twenty-eight, I knew I faced a serious choice. If I did not take one of the offers coming my way from the sweet but uninspiring men I dated, I would soon be left high and dry. . . . I took a look around at who I wanted to spend time with over the next fifty to sixty years. . . . It wasn't any of the men who were courting me. It was the girls I spent time with who, like me, were reluctant to become what a wife was expected to be in 1935.

Living in a marriage-focused society, these women have often felt the need to justify their single status—to establish that they really aren't strange. They substantiate maternal instincts by doting over nieces and nephews, and assert their femininity by telling stories of enviable romantic adventures. Or they might tell a story of deep family dedication, like Gertie, seventy-eight, who spent her middle years taking care of her aging parents:

I couldn't have lived with myself if I hadn't done my bit to care for them. They needed me, and I couldn't in my right mind leave them. My sisters had their hands full with children and husbands. If they could care for me in my first seventeen years, it seemed fair that I should care for them in their last days.

While Gertie says she has no regrets and wouldn't have done it any other way, nonetheless part of her own social development and mobility were blocked. She lacks that unique blend of self-reliance and dependence that so characterizes women who have consciously constructed their own social and emotional lives. These women, like Gretchen, eighty-five, a dancer, cat breeder, and member of a rich community of friends, have developed both a capacity to rely on others as well as a robust independence.

Women who embrace being single have lived in many times and places. They can be the proud Suffragist Spinsters of the 19th Century, feisty Japanese young professionals who call their own shots with "gaijin" males, Mayans so embedded in their extended families that their husbandlessness produces no more than a shrug and a giggle, Russian women whose out-of-wedlock maternity was fully supported socially, legally, and financially, or today's older Americans, who defied all odds and fashioned just the social and emotional lives they wanted. Their stories affirm that if you are a single woman, you certainly are not alone. With such a rich precedence for fulfillment, you, too, can feel assured that you can have everything you want. But if you still have the nagging sense that something's missing, read on to the next chapter, as we unravel the predicament of "Women Who Have Almost Everything."

Chapter 3

WOMEN WHO HAVE ALMOST EVERYTHING

❦ • ❦

FACING ALONENESS

*D*iane, forty-two and unmarried, opens an envelope from her credit card company. No, it isn't a bill. It's an offer to purchase low-cost life insurance. "What do I need that for?" she groans. Diane pays her own rent and bills, and her parents are likely to die before she does. A lump lodges in her chest as she realizes, "There's no one who depends on me—no one will really need me if I go."

Never before have there been so many financially and socially self-contained women. And never before have they had such trepidation about growing close to others. These women, from their anxious twenties through their near-devastating late thirties, forties, and fifties, have everything but intimacy. These are women like Gina, twenty-eight, who after years of roommates and live-in boyfriends, took the plunge and rented her own one-bedroom apartment.

For the first several weeks, she was in ecstasy, able to design her living space just the way she saw fit. For once she didn't need to think about anyone else. When she had no idea what she wanted, memories of the years of compromising with others surfaced. Sweat evaporated as she gazed at blank walls that she could leave blank as long as she cared to.

Once she put everything in place, an eerie calm set in. No one was there to greet her when she came home at the end of the day, no one wished her good morning or good night. . . . She was really alone.

For two solid weeks, she cried each time she'd unlock the front door and sense the emptiness of her place. Would this pain ever go away? True, she could wear anything she wanted (or nothing at all) any time of day or night, she could take noisy showers at 3 a.m. or make ten phone calls in a row, but this was hardly a trade-off.

Christine, beautiful, smart, accomplished, and forty-three, is far from Gina's teary, first-stage empty-house loneliness. Hers is much more insidious. Recently, she finished a mid-career master's degree from Harvard's Kennedy School of Government and returned to her comfortable Seattle home and a $75,000-a-year position in public administration. Christine is a living testament to the fact that the more education and prestige a woman has, the more likely she will be single.

In her last twenty-five years of men and romance, she'd certainly seemed to have had it all. She'd had solid, enduring relationships, great sex, and good communication. There was nothing wrong with her nor with the men that she met. So why is this woman who loves to cook and keeps a warm, bright house with a couple of cute cats not married? Moreover, why is not being married so painful to her?

Over the last eight years, Christine nurtured a relationship with a man who, from the day they met, told her that he had no interest in marrying again. She believed she could change his mind. She liked him a lot and was so accustomed to getting everything she wanted, she figured she'd eventually get him, too. On second thought, some of what she liked about the last eight years was that she really wasn't in a relationship. Because he was often at just a low simmer in her life, she had tremendous freedom, to do what she wanted, whenever she wanted to.

All her friends who were once part of her social world are now wrapped up in family life. Christine cringes at the thought of doing something just to meet a guy, like running a personals ad in the *Seattle Weekly*, or joining a video dating service. However lonely she feels, in her mind, going around the block even one more time would be totally pointless. Tears roll from her eyes as she contemplates the prospect of being very alone for the rest of her life.

THE TIGHT SHIP

While some people may go from one relationship to another, barely spending a moment on their own, many of the women I interviewed had perfected the art of being single. They are dedicated professionals who own homes and take full responsibility for their own economic, social, and emotional well-being. While potential partners might view them as "controlling" and "emotionally unavailable," these women feel their very survival depends on running a tight ship.

Arlene, forty-one, is a research scientist at the Nuclear Regulatory Commission in Washington, D.C. She travels on business frequently and works well over forty hours a week when she's in town. She owns a beautiful home in a Virginia suburb, and whenever she has a weekend in town, she stays home, eats popcorn for dinner, and putters.

While Arlene says she'd like to meet a man, her commitments make it next to impossible. Her social world is composed largely of co-workers, who join her for quick lunches and/or travel assignments. The men on these teams are usually married, while the women, like herself, are self-contained professionals who run their own tight ships.

As for Arlene's prospects, there are certainly single professional men in D.C., but their focus is generally on work, not relationships. If they are in politics, they're forever on a deadline and/or trying to keep up with breaking news. As one woman reported, "These guys are more inclined to stay up to watch *Nightline* than to romance a woman."

I also saw this self-absorption in Linda, a thirty-nine-year-old Washington, D.C., accountant. While her job isn't as time consuming as Arlene's, she, too, runs a very tight ship. She has had the same Capitol neighborhood apartment for the last twelve years. And her apartment is as orderly as her life. She rises early for a morning jog, catches the subway to arrive at work before 8 a.m., usually stays in for lunch, gets off in time to fix a quick dinner, and then goes off to an evening class. Her schedule and interests are so fixed that nobody is ever able to disrupt them.

When visitors come to town, she gladly gives them maps and advice, but never joins them. Nothing, and certainly not a man, could convince her to surrender to other aesthetics and appetites. Like a spayed cat in its home territory, she has absolutely no interest in wandering.

I had no idea how tight my own ship was until I began seeing Don. I was so accustomed to thinking in terms of "me" that transitioning to "we" caused intense turbulence. Rather than raising a concern and discussing how we might solve it together, I was forever proclaiming decisions. I was so used to calling all the shots in my life that my notion of including him was largely telling him what I wanted. I didn't (without some concerted work) consider what he wanted—I only knew what I could handle.

I learned that knowing what I wanted to do wasn't enough. It wasn't going to make him feel we were creating a relationship together. While he might very well enjoy attending all the things I wanted to attend, I had to present them to him as options rather than requirements. Rather than proclaiming, "I'm going over to Warren and Rae's tonight and you're welcome to join us if you want to," I had to learn to reframe it into an opportunity for us both to consider. Thinking in terms of "we," I'd pose, "Warren and Rae wanted to know if we'd like to come over this evening. What do you think?" This way Don could be a thinking, breathing, loving member of a relationship rather than the male object Leanna drags around to her already prescribed activities. Ultimately, much of what I wanted to do he did, too—as long as I made him party to the planning.

Women on their own often have good, solid self-protective reasons for putting together a tight ship, and abandoning it is never easy. Nonetheless, the rewards can be rich and wonderful once you let go enough to co-create rather than always digging your heels in to proclaim!

THE CREATION OF SELF AS A DEFENSE

More than anything, Austrian-born Audrey, fifty-four, wants a man. In defense, she's created a self that's so substantial materially, she could take care of herself forever. Nonetheless, this hard-headed Hollywood media producer says she'd readily trade her fur coat collection, Malibu townhouse, and late-model Mercedes for a simple life filled with one man's unconditional love.

Despite her desperate moans and groans, when Audrey recites what she's acquired through her own brilliance and hard work, I sense her pride in being a self-made woman. Many women cling with all their bull-headed strength to the self they've created as a defense against ordinariness. If there is no constant man in their life to adore them each day for just being, they make themselves extraordinary.

Lindy, thirty-nine, while lacking Audrey's business sense, has made her body the masterpiece. She works out daily with a personal trainer, had the most perfect breast implants well before the silicone fear hit the press, is planning a nose job, and sports a gorgeous bronzed mane with just the right touch of blonde highlights. She is her appearance. Even when dating doesn't lead to a relationship (and despite her unending optimism, it rarely does), she walks away confident, knowing her body is beautiful.

Joanne, thirty-one, can endure manlessness because she knows she has an extraordinary brain. She buries herself each night and just about every weekend in her doctoral dissertation. Her small house shows few signs of life other than a whirring computer, stacks of paper and books distributed in mazes only she can decipher. Her answering machine is full of messages she may never get around to returning. As long as her literature search can be appended and her data run through several yet-to-be refined programs, she can put off questions about men, intimacy, and loneliness.

Unlike these women who have created extraordinary selves, other women simply put huge chunks of their social-emotional centers on hold. Rather than straining themselves to be a somebody, they wallow in the "I Need My Love Nest Syndrome." They put off buying the match-ing linens and the silverware they really want, preferring to hide out as college student vagabonds. Because they aren't decorating their homes with a true love, the walls remain bare and the cabinets empty. They feel like a zero alone.

CAUSES OF COLLAPSE

Much of what causes collapse for the woman who has almost everything is rooted in fragile self-esteem. The ever-confident career woman who routinely calls all the shots may melt into a helpless lump if one raw nerve is exposed.

Breaking up, or facing what once seemed like a "this-is-it relationship," can be one of the bigger blows for the woman who is on the way to hav-ing everything. As Gloria Steinem noted in *Revolution from Within: A Book of Self-Esteem*, the solid exterior of this kind of woman may hide a self-esteem that is determined more by the state of her love life than her own con-scious life creations. Gerri, a gregarious and highly successful publicist, crumbles to nothingness when a man she's interested in fails to call:

> *It's like I want to disappear—I hate what I do so much! The last time this hap-pened, I was dating this man named Scott, who, I'll have to admit, must have been pretty ambivalent. Anyways, I would sit in a lump on the couch wrapped*

in a blanket waiting for the damn phone to ring. I'd just stare into the walls and wait. I couldn't eat, couldn't go outside, and couldn't call anybody else. After one of my waiting spells, I got so frustrated, I finally dialed his number. When he answered he barely said "boo." He expressed no interest in getting together, and then I really went down the tubes. . . .

While Gerri falls apart over phone calls not received, many women like Riane, a newspaper journalist, get men to fall in love with them to feel validated:

On my own, I'm okay, sometimes a little low, mostly just even and okay. Then, last year when I met Stu, my whole sense of self-worth changed. He wanted to hear about every story I wrote, about every person I met, and probably about every thought I had. Each week, he'd send flowers to my office, and several times a day he'd call just to see how I was doing. I felt so special!

Riane readily admits that the best part about having Stu fall in love with her was how special it made her feel. Stu could have been anybody. She drew him in to raise her own self-esteem, not to have a conscious relationship. When he assessed how much she was taking, how little she was giving, and ultimately how uninspired she was to give anything to him, he backed off. She concluded:

When Stu said he loved me, I felt better about myself. I wasn't just this plain-looking beat reporter, but I was this very special, very desired person. Every word I uttered, every thought I shared had value because he noticed. After a while, I found myself embellishing my own little thoughts and experiences so there'd more to share with him.

Then, when he said he wanted me to put more into the relationship and I couldn't muster up a sincere interest in him, I felt like such a self-serving bitch.

Their love affair over, Riane still feels guilty:

Now that it's over, I feel horrible about myself. All his interest in me wasn't really in me, Riane, the amazing woman, it was in having a relationship with me, Riane, the potential life partner. So, I let him use me for his fantasy, so I could feel better about myself. Right now I feel worse about myself than I did before I ever met him. I wish I could love myself in such a way that I don't use men for that.

While Riane smarts from the backfire of inviting a man into her life that she never really loved, Erica, a highly skilled psychotherapist, tears herself apart over breaking up with a man she really wanted to love:

> *I really thought Jesse and I would work it out. We were honest, shared feelings, discussed our dreams, and had such fun together. We liked the same foods, had similar aesthetics, and my cat even like him. . . .*
>
> *At some point the little boy in him that had been abandoned by women started getting very jealous of my time. I had an extremely heavy client load and wasn't able to give him the assurance he so desperately needed. Then he started to tear me apart. . . . There was nothing I could do to reassure him.*
>
> *I started feeling horrible. Like me, Erica, this so-called expert in relationships who other people pay $100 an hour for her wisdom, is really very messed up. I feared that deep inside, after all of those superficial brilliant layers get worn through, that I was a disaster. I got to the point where it was beyond me to work it out with him and the thought of ever working it out with any man at all just seemed preposterous.*

Like Erica, a woman who bases her self-worth on her ability to have a loving relationship is bound to feel low when her efforts fail. Glenda, unlike Erica, Riane, and Gerri, used her collapse-triggering incident, a car accident, as an opportunity for recentering and growth:

> *My doctor told me I was an accident waiting to happen. I had so much rage in me before the actual crash that getting hit simply provided an opportunity to let it out. Initially I was angry at the other driver, at cars in general, insurance adjusters, auto body shops, and at my own body for taking so long to heal.*
>
> *Then, while lying in bed, trying to heal, I came to realize what really was broken. I had never been loved. My family had always criticized me and I never stood up to them. And the men I'd pick pretty much did the same thing. Gradually, I began healing my self-esteem.*
>
> *The more I loved myself, the less what other people thought mattered. With my*

newfound strength, I stood up to my family . . . and never again have they even tried to tear me apart. As for men, I'm open, but I feel so whole in myself that I know I don't need to be in a relationship with a guy to feel complete. . . .

PUTTING *RELATIONSHIP* ON A PEDESTAL

In a gender-polarized culture like ours, we put relationship-romance on a pedestal. We value "falling in love" and read self-help authors like Ellen Kreidman to avert the inevitable displacement of intense romance by calm familiarity. We are most prone to falling in love when we feel vulnerable and wish to be magically rescued. For some women, bottom-line survival skills involve getting a man to fall in love with them.

Jan, thirty-five, was at wit's end when she took a job as a waitress at a military base coffee shop. She had two estranged husbands fighting for custody of her baby girl and toddler son. Broke, she wanted desperately to keep her children and her freedom. Her solution came in the form of a gangling military officer named Dale. She delivered an intensity that caused him to pull all the stops, and within two weeks, marry her. Suddenly, Jan and her kids were settled into on-base housing and reaping the benefits of a military family. When Dale was transferred to Germany, Jan barely batted an eye. She opted to send him off on his own.

Relationship gets put on a pedestal by many of the single people who attend workshops, seminars, and support groups for perfecting their interpersonal skills. Many of the most popular of these seminars focus on sexy topics like flirting, how to create instant rapport, how to attract women/men, the art of courtship and seduction, how to strip for your lover, and how to drive your woman wild in bed. The undercurrent of these alluring subjects is basically how to get lots of hot sex while staying single and fancy-free. Perfecting any of these skills would more than likely *detract* from one's ability to nurture and keep a relationship.

The strategies offered in such seminars (and others we'll discuss in Chapter Five) are largely training for presenting an unauthentic self. They can wreak havoc when the other party isn't practicing a workshop-endorsed strategy. Deena had no idea what she was getting into when she accepted a date with Mitch, a graduate of a power-dating seminar. Mitch had learned to focus on the woman while revealing as little as possible about himself. His mission, his seminar leader advised, was to stay in control and gather the data he needed to make a level-headed assessment regarding whether he'd like to pursue an intimate relationship. Deena, meanwhile, found him to be distant, stilted, and altogether unreal:

For our first date, he told me nothing about what was planned other than to wear either a miniskirt or jeans, bring a jacket, and be ready at seven. The evening was filled with one weird mystery after another. At one point he pulled the car into a little park and we played croquet for twenty minutes, then we walked around this lake and fed the ducks, and then we sat under a tree and he pulled out a couple of sandwiches and we ate them.

Now, I'm not saying I don't enjoy surprises, but that's all it was. He said just about nothing about himself. By the end of the evening, I didn't know his age, the kind of work he did, anything about his dreams, anything about his past, nor anything about his passions. While he looked alive, he certainly didn't act alive!

Deena grew increasingly frustrated as she weathered several more dates filled with little surprises and virtually no personal disclosure. To me, this "dating strategy" made no sense unless there were women who had undergone a companion seminar titled something like "Give Him the Power and Enjoy the Mystery." Then, a full courtship dance might occur.

Lucky for my investigation, I did track down a cluster of women who had taken the companion seminar (it had a much less obnoxious name than the one I invented). These women, being unilaterally bruised by disclosing too much to men, claimed to very much like dates that were lighthearted and mysterious. Being equally anxious about giving up their power, dating without disclosure made good sense to them. But Deena and Mitch's only area of convergence was personal chemistry. Rather than fueling deeper intimacy and trust, it fueled confusion and distrust. After a while, the only reason Deena accepted Mitch's invitations was because he turned her on. Their connection quickly became a purely sexual one. Because he subscribed to the values of his seminar and she refused to make herself into a "give-him-the-power-and-enjoy-the-mystery" groupie, their attempt at a relationship collapsed.

Deena's experience with Mitch confirms that strategizing the intimacy-building process and then revering the relationship as an intangible goal are the onerous outcomes of codifying and depersonalizing an otherwise dynamic process.

Averting The Pain

Many women do not do well with the freedom they have acquired. Once isolated in their private homes, condos and apartments, free to make their own schedules and arrangements, loneliness may set in.

Tasks that may take an otherwise fulfilled person a couple of hours can take a pain-averter all weekend to procrastinate and another week to finish. When single people sense that they are really on their own, they may avert this loneliness and pain by getting very busy. A busy schedule helps them feel needed, if not important.

Lora, a vivacious mother of two grown sons, works as a film production coordinator more to distract herself from deep loneliness than to pay the bills. She can better handle the nagging pressure and long hours at work than she can the nagging loneliness and long nights at home.

The best part of my job is that it's very social. I'm always on the phone, in meetings, or running out to look things over or pick things up. I rarely have a moment to myself. I like it that way.

Whenever we go on hiatus, it's the pits. I'm not interested in spending time by myself or meeting friends for tea or lunch or something like that. I like feeling needed. And I hate filling up my time with little social visits rather than working on real projects.

Pain-averters may construct elaborate social networks, keeping in touch with scores of friends on a near-daily basis, date five people at once and squeeze every possible social gathering into their ultra-busy schedules. Or they may make themselves indispensable at work. Doreen, forty-one, energetically attends singles parties every night of the week that she isn't out on a date. When asked how long she can keep her optimism going, she says, "A couple more years . . . by forty-five, if I'm not married, I think I'll just stop." She pauses, holds her breath a second and forces a smile. "No one can say I didn't try."

Certain that she doesn't want a family, Doreen passionately wants a husband. Over the last five years, she's been in and out of relationships lasting anywhere from two to nine months. Ever confident, she's often brimming with a "this-could-be-it" story. And when it doesn't work out, as is usually the case, she expertly patches up her raging loneliness with more parties, more hours at the gym, more hours on the phone with her girlfriends, and as soon as she feels ready, more dating. Lora and Doreen, each with their different strategies, are dodging the pain of being emotionally very alone.

Phyllis, sensing her need to be part of a social world and exhausted by "dating that never leads to intimacy," decided to befriend couples and their children:

Since I see myself as a "person" first and "single" perhaps tenth, I decided to befriend couples and their kids, rather than dating needy dreary single men. This way I could avoid the all-or-nothing judgments and simply get together for pleasant visits.

While Phyllis' intentions seemed honorable, being single in a couples/family world proved to be problematic. While her goal was to become part of a group and to feel accepted for just who she is, the couples often treated her as a diversion from their workaday lives. When she came by, they expected to be entertained by her stories of dating and being a woman on her own. Often, the wives felt threatened. They wondered if she was getting along too well with their husbands. According to Phyllis:

I had absolutely no interest in rocking the boat, I was just rock-bottom lonely. One night, I was over at these friends' house and it got real late. Now, I know if I had to, I could have driven home. But when the husband suggested I stay over, I relished the opportunity. I was so tired of waking up alone and having the only sound I heard be a refrigerator hum. I so wanted to hear the sounds of other people that I gladly snuggled into their lumpy couch.

In the morning, it got a little weird because the husband wanted me to hang out and talk while the wife kept trying to end our conversation and get me out of there. I really had no interest in taking him away from her, I was just really, really lonely, and it was so nice to read the paper and have morning coffee with someone.

Nonetheless, Phyllis persisted in befriending couples. Another couple, Rich and Celeste, while plenty entertaining and engaging on their own, felt the need to have their connection with Phyllis be something productive and purposeful. Phyllis recalls:

Then suddenly out of nowhere Rich asked me, "What do you want?" I thought about it and basically said, "I just want all of us to get closer and grow into good friends." Then I realized that these two were very interested in helping entrepreneurs launch new businesses. If I could figure out a business that they could help me with, or find one of theirs that I could help them with, then we'd be in each other's social worlds. Otherwise, I'd be history.

From the inside out, from the vantage point of being in a loving relationship may be when we can best appreciate how we avert the pain of being alone. Lynne was astounded by how much patching up and numbing out of raw loneliness she had been doing until she got into a serious relationship:

I had no idea how lonely I had been until I started getting close to Peter. Then, I realized how much of my running to parties, lectures, and workshops, was simply a way to be around people. It was rare that I met anyone I liked, so it wasn't really to meet somebody, it was just to avoid feeling so lonely. God, I remember staying out so late that after driving home on what must have been "automatic pilot," I'd sit in the car for five or ten minutes, just trying to wake up enough to let myself into the house.

While Lynne now finds tremendous pleasure in quiet evenings alone with just Peter, for many single women juggling, displacing, replacing, dodging, gathering, infusing, and running are at best piecemeal attempts to belong and feel human, especially when Prince Charming may no longer be just around the corner.

Women who have almost everything are caught in a culture warp. The family has changed, and what used to draw men and women together now barely exists. Instead, the gender realities of being a single woman of means are often a horrible mismatch to a single man who seeks a relationship. The women, independent and self-aware, as well as damaged and guarded, tend to find partners who are mirrors of themselves, rather than their childhood dream. When they can't find a flexible, attractive, generous, healthy man, they promulgate activity to numb their own deep loneliness. For some women, their noisily ticking bio-time-clocks trigger their choices in how to address loneliness, belonging, mothering, mortality, and commitment. In the next chapter, we will explore these "Bio-Time-Clock Women."

Chapter 4

Bio-Time-Clock Women

\~•✓

*T*he pressure to become a mother can sometimes feel stronger than the pressure to marry. This ***bio-time-clock pressure*** is fueled by the loss of fertility following menopause. Our rigid and hypocritical culture prescribes the nuclear family as the bastion of child conception, and children conceived by unknown fathers have been denigrated as "bastards." While countries such as Finland provide full financial and social support to children, regardless of the whereabouts of their fathers, here we shun huge social sectors by enforcing "nuclear family values." Despite all of these cultural strictures, in some of our cities, babies born to single mothers account for fifty percent of all births.

According to the Census Bureau Report, "Fertility of American Women June 1992," since 1982 out-of-wedlock births have increased in every region of the country with a sixty percent increase overall. Growth in single motherhood has been particularly sharp among white, affluent and educated women. Single women with at least a year of college had an 11.3% pregnancy rate, more than double the 1982 figure of 5.5%.

BIO-TIME-CLOCK FRENZY

I never thought I'd become a bio-time-clock woman because I was always interested in having children. In my late twenties, I wrote a guide to birth options and then went on to produce an award-winning documentary on natural childbirth. Back then, I would lie awake designing the perfect pregnancy, birth and parenting experience. Though I drifted through my twenties and then all of my thirties without having children, I knew it wasn't for lack of interest in being a mother.

Then, one week into being forty, I had a conversation with a man that hurled me into the midst of "bio-time-clock frenzy." Contending that a forty-year-old woman is too old to have children, he proclaimed:

> First she'd have to get into the right relationship with the right guy, then they'd need several years to build a history together. Then, perhaps in her mid-forties, she'd try to have kids, though by then her advanced age would make conception pretty unlikely. If she did manage to give birth, she'd be a lousy mother, because she'd be too wrapped up in her own life and own career. . . .

I turned pale and nearly wept as this man wagged his finger across my face, warning, "a forty-year-old woman can be a wonderful lover, but she should stay away from being a mother." I pulled myself together, stomped out of his house and immediately started scheming about how to have children before my bio-time-clock stopped ticking.

For Carmen, twenty-eight, a portentous gynecological exam propelled her into "bio-time-clock frenzy." When a doctor diagnosed her with cervical cancer, Carmen lapsed into deep depression. She had presumed she'd have eight to ten more years to gradually build a relationship with a "Mr. Right" before getting pregnant. Carmen felt her future was on the line:

> It's like I'm no longer perfect—I'm damaged goods, and no one is going to want to be with me. I'll suffer alone, totally destroyed, never having had children, never marrying. I feel so desperately alone!

For Helen, forty-two, "bio-time-clock frenzy" was triggered by her thirty-seven-year-old boyfriend's reluctance to agree to marry her and start a family before the end of the year. As her clock ticks toward its eleventh hour, she thinks how unfair it is that men don't have biological time clocks. They can just about put off fathering forever while she must weigh her alternatives. Should she buy sperm and have a child on her own or can she count on her commitment-shy boyfriend to step into her plan?

Once the belle of some of San Francisco's hottest parties in the '60s and '70s, Helen is astonished to be in this position. Her warmth, beauty and honesty had filled her communal house in Haight-Ashbury with one hot romance after another. After years of barely making ends meet, she stabilized her finances by becoming a public-health nurse. She calculates that if she gets pregnant in the next year, she can buy a small house in which to raise the baby she so desperately wants.

Is she really ready to give up most of her freedom to raise a child on her own? She nods "yes," explaining:

> There really aren't any more jazz clubs to go to that I haven't been to at least twenty times. No one's having parties, I don't like eating out that much anymore. . . . In fact I spend several nights a week at home alone and it's really okay. I don't feel like I'm missing anything.

BECOMING A SINGLE MOTHER BY CHOICE

Bio-time-clock women such as Helen and Carmen make a deal with themselves, with nature and with the men in their lives. Under pressure, they carve out a future that offers bits and pieces of their '50s-inspired fantasy of a blissful mother with child.

Denise, thirty-eight, a native of Ohio, made one such deal. Three years ago she became pregnant by her twenty-nine-year-old lover. He wanted her to get an abortion. Facing what might be her last chance to become a mom, she opted to keep the baby. Her lover moved on, and now her life consists of full-time work, grocery shopping, a couple of hours in the evenings with her daughter, and sleep. On weekends, she runs errands, takes her daughter to the park, and that's all. She hasn't been out to dinner or to a party since her daughter's birth. The sum total of her last year's recreation consisted of two movies on New Year's Day.

Listening to Denise's story, I sensed that despite her determination to have a child, she was certainly not a self-absorbed corporate go-getter who pursues everything she wants. Denise, like most of the single mothers by choice I interviewed, tends to be quite traditional; she just really wanted a child—so much so that she willingly dragged herself and her baby into near-poverty to do it. Asked if she's frustrated, exhausted and in need of a husband, she grins:

> Yes, but I wouldn't have it any other way. My daughter has brought such joy to my life—you wouldn't know unless you'd had one. . . . She's really filled in all my cracks.

Women who get accidentally pregnant and want to keep the child don't have a particularly good reputation in our society. They are typically young and shortsighted, hoping perhaps for increased involvement with the father. If the boyfriend refuses this pressure to marry, typically, the single mothers burden their own families or the welfare system.

There are alternatives for healthy, responsible, educated bio-time-clock women besides floating into some bar, meeting a guy, claiming she's on the pill and then later slapping him with a paternity suit. She could do what Stephanie, forty-seven, did fourteen years ago. Then thirty-three and a social worker, she had a brief affair with a old friend which led to a healthy baby boy. She surmises:

> *I could never have forgiven myself if I had gotten too old to have a child. You know, in life there are no guarantees—I might have looked forever for Mr. Right and never gotten pregnant and never had a child. My need was to have a child. It was my project—my adventure. I did it and I'm doing it and I'm proud!*

Once her pregnancy was under way, Stephanie found that she had very little interest in an ongoing relationship with her old friend. What she had wanted (and what she got) was to be a mother. While she has endeavored to bring father figures into her child's life, working full-time and being a mother has limited her time for or interest in finding a suitable husband.

Her son, Eric, however, sees it differently. And his perception is what makes conceiving a child with an uninterested father so problematic. Eric feels abandoned by his father. He wants this man, who never openly consented to be his biological father, to recognize him and love him. And the father refuses. He contends that Stephanie conned him, and he wants nothing more to do with her nor with Eric, the product of the con.

Eric can't understand why he was conceived if his father never wanted him. With Eric's dilemma in mind, I set out to do better. I wanted my child to be conceived by a consenting man who would openly and lovingly father my child.

FINDING A FATHER/CO-PARENT

Thus my adventure began. I quickly came to realize that in our culture, there are few precedents for upstanding educated women to have out-of-wedlock children with upstanding educated men. Rather than being encouraged and applauded, my motives were meanspiritedly dissected: Was I sure I didn't just want another cat or a new car? Advice was freely dispensed: Perhaps I should move to Alaska or Australia, where loving father-objects presumably abound.

The qualities I found attractive in men started to shift. My penchant for playful, wild, sexy, self-absorbed intellectual powerhouses gave way to guys with good genes, good hearts and good credit. I devised what could be best described as my "Co-Parenting Wish List." Here, I laid out what I wanted:

1. A loving conception – preceded by tests for HIV and other sexually transmitted diseases
2. Emotional and possible financial support during pregnancy and postpartum
3. Attendance at the birth
4. Inclusion of the man's name as father on the birth certificate
5. An ongoing social relationship with the child
6. Agreement to be life-long co-parents with shared custody and shared decision making.

As I discussed the ramifications of this wish list with potential co-parents, I began to comprehend that this arrangement portended to be as messy and complicated as a surrogate mother contract plus a post-divorce custody agreement. Despite whatever promises I and a prospective father might make, the law could always override us.

For example, when filling out the forms for the child's birth certificate, I could designate anyone I chose (including someone who was clearly not the biological father or nobody at all). But a child holds the right to be maintained by its legal father, and likewise should the father become impoverished, he would hold the right to be maintained by the child. A legal father is considered financially responsible to his child until the day he goes to court and brings in evidence (like DNA test results) to prove that he is not the child's biological father.

If no one were designated as father on a child's birth certificate, at some later date DNA testing could be done to establish the biological father's paternity. This evidence could then be brought to court to establish this man as the legal father, with all rights and obligations.

As I sought to become a mother in a responsible, non-manipulative way, I was horrified by how thoroughly the contentious proto-fathers scrutinized my desires. What if they didn't approve of the medical or day care, or the schools or the vacations I arranged for this yet-to-be conceived child? What would I do? What would they do? Why did they care so much? Why was I asking anyone to openly father my child?

I sat quietly with myself and took stock of my offers:

1. Gay and bisexual men who had no interest or expectation to ever develop a deep relationship with a woman.
2. Men who were so impoverished that they would have nothing to lose in a paternity suit.
3. Men who are happy with multiple partners (and don't particularly want a permanent relationship), but who still yearn for a biological child that they wouldn't have to be particularly responsible for.

Finally, I had to admit to myself that I wanted to have fun co-parenting. And none of these guys exuded the kind of social energy I was interested in exchanging. I wanted the man who fathers my children to love me unconditionally. I didn't want him to be so suspicious of my motives and to have so little to offer.

Jannie, forty-two and a massage therapist, heard about my search for the right father and confided she was looking for one, too. After discussing the attributes of the men on our "short lists" (mine were wild and sexy and perhaps had good genes, while hers looked homely but had big hearts), we schemed about living together. This way we could spell each other off for babysitting, cooking and cleaning. It would certainly be better than being isolated, overworked, nearly impoverished single mothers. But did we really want to settle for a cluttered house and borderline poverty? While I dreamed about making millions being a pop anthropologist/writer, she looked us both over and concluded that to do this well, we'd need up-front money.

We realized that we'd been approaching motherhood with a poverty consciousness. Since we hadn't found loving worker-bee husbands, we presumed we'd have to foot the whole bill. Our consciousness changed when we heard about Rachel, who had contracted with wealthy industrialist Stephen to be the mother of his children. Stephen provided Rachel with sperm, a house and full financial support in exchange for her being a devoted and loving mother to his (and her) children. The arrangement didn't really didn't seem that extraordinary to us. Traditional husbands routinely support their wives. The only real difference is that Rachel and Stephen live separately and are each free to have separate romantic lives, much as Britain's Princess Di and Prince Charles do. Moreover, divorced fathers are often expected to provide some variation of this arrangement for their ex-wives.

Other countries and cultures commonly separate relationships for procreation from romance. The Wadabe of Africa make clear distinctions between who they love and who they share a home with. A married man will openly and fervently pursue a woman for love even if he has several wives at home. While his social and economic identity is wrapped up with his wives, everyone honors and respects his need to find love.

In many European and Latin American countries, wealthy men openly have mistresses. The mistresses are aware of the wives, and the wives are equally aware of the mistresses. Each has a recognized role in the man's life. And the women themselves may parallel these arrangements with their own lovers/husbands.

Westerners, however, have endeavored to fuse love and marriage since sometime around the 14th century, when courtly love (passionate romantic love for that deeply desired and delectable courtesan) was outlawed by the church. Ordinary procreation-based marriage was sanctified as love's bastion. Though marriage may have been prevented the spread of venereal diseases in the Middle Ages, and insured paternity rights and obligations, it has also proven to be at best cumbersome and at worst impossible.

Then why did I have such a hard time finding a suitable co-parent? Despite all of my historical and cross cultural information about separating procreation from romance, I had to admit that it was very difficult for me to consider co-parenting with someone I didn't love. The only men I sincerely wanted as co-parents were men I could easily imagine marrying.

Co-parenting challenges our belief in the multi-dimensional nature of romantic relationships. When we love someone very deeply, we want to have a baby with them—we are very comfortable about producing a "love child". Meanwhile, just the thought of a man and woman agreeing to produce and love a child without any intention of every loving each other makes us very uncomfortable. Given the fact that many of today's children are co-parented by their once-married mothers and fathers, we shouldn't dismiss this possibility too quickly. There is a logic to co-parenting: one can focus just on a parenting relationship and not be burdened by the exigencies of a full-blown romantic commitment that might involve sexuality, deep emotions, housekeeping, and fully shared social and economic lives.

SECURING A SPERM DONATION

Exhausted by the prospect of finding a good co-parent, I drew up a fathering agreement in which I kept all control and basically accepted a sperm donation. Even then, my openness drew flack. Could I assure the potential fathers that I would never ever sue them for paternity? Suddenly the life-giving qualities of fertile, sperm-rich semen took on powerful importance. This same substance that women who are sexual with men have had deposited on their chests and their faces and inside of every willing orifice and have then felt dribble down their legs as if there was just too much of it and they'd never ever feel clean again was now intensely valuable and had to be protected. If it had to be protected, why do most heterosexual men dispense it so freely to women?

In some cultures, men are extremely protective of their semen as a matter of course. Practitioners of tantric yoga in India are trained to bring their orgasmic sensations to a higher level so that ejaculation is not part of the sexual act. In the mid-1800s utopian Oneida community in upstate New York, the men practiced coitus reservatus, wherein sexual intercourse did not include ejaculation. Thus the children who were conceived were planned and wanted by all.

Here in the U.S., we are living a contradiction. Men freely dispense sperm, but are intensely concerned about giving life to children they have not approved of. Perhaps their only recourse is to get a vasectomy, or routinely use double condoms and then tie them up and take them home so no devious lover will reach into the wastebasket and undo them once he leaves. A woman who wants sperm will find it. . . . And according to law, if she wants to sue for paternity payments, she can do that, too.

Eventually, I found I could persuade just about every man I knew (married or not) to anonymously donate sperm to me if I promised to tell the rest of the world I had conceived the child through a sperm bank. I decided to expand my data base by surveying about 200 of my anthropology students, ranging in age from eighteen to fifty-five.

The males were divided on whether they would agree to be social fathers to children resulting from accidental pregnancies. Some claimed they would persuade the woman to have an abortion, and if she wouldn't, they'd disappear. Others saw the disappearing act as horribly callous and said they'd do whatever they could, including marry the woman. One told me unplanned pregnancies had happened to him twice, and both times he married the woman! I wondered what kind of sensors a desperate bio-time-clock woman would need to find a guy like him.

Men were on the whole suspicious of a woman who directly asked for a sperm donation. They feared legal and financial entrapment, the loss of a "true family life" and lack of control over the child's upbringing. If they thought the woman would be financially responsible and would make a good mother, they might acquiesce. Others didn't like the idea of not being full-time fathers to their biological children. One guy admitted privately that a lesbian couple had asked him to father a child for each of them and he wasn't sure what he'd do. (I think he was mostly relieved to find out he wasn't the only one on the planet being made such an offer.)

Finally, I asked the women if they'd allow their husbands or boyfriends to father another woman's child. The majority of the women were dead-set against it. They feared their man's time and attentions would become divided and there would be less left for them. Finally, one married woman did volunteer her husband, noting that sex with him would be much safer than with a disease-carrying bar patron.

THE SPERM BANK OPTION

An option that's even cleaner than this woman's sparkling husband would be to purchase anonymously donated frozen sperm. While sperm banks were perhaps designed to assist married women whose husbands are infertile or genetically deficient, now about forty percent of the users of the California Cryobank are single women. After being subjected to exhaustingly intense scrutiny and dissection by several prospective fathers, I came to realize why many single women in our culture prefer to buy anonymous sperm. The message rang clearly: Interpersonal negotiations regarding procreation can be so overwhelming that the only condition under which most of us would navigate through them is the total trust that comes when we're "in love."

For $133 a cubic centimeter of sperm (not a full ejaculation, but enough to achieve conception), Cryobank patrons can pick through donations from over 200 college student donors, representing a variety of ethnic and racial backgrounds. For each donor, a family health history and genetic overview is available. Because frozen sperm are a little less motile than sperm found in fresh, warm ejaculate, conception may not occur until the fifth or sixth try. While records are routinely sealed, a donor can agree to allow his biological child to contact him once the child turns eighteen.

The sperm and donors themselves are run through a full battery of tests, assuring a level of safety well beyond most traditional conceptions. For added security, fully tested sperm is banked for six months prior to being dispensed. There is also a personal donor program, wherein I could instruct my donor of choice to submit to every known test ever devised for a father-to-be. I then asked, "After the prescribed six-month wait, if he were certified clean, could I just take him home and lure out my own fresh sample?" The bank technician nearly went into shock thinking about the diseases I was willing to risk by subjecting myself to fresh semen. If sanitized sperm banking represents the wave of future, I just may not be ready.

HIGH-TECH POST-MENOPAUSAL OPTIONS

Other than sperm banking, what else can medical technology offer the woman who wants to buy more time on her bio-time-clock? It's been demonstrated that a post-menopausal woman with an intact uterus can receive an embryo, carry it for a full-term pregnancy and deliver it, too. That embryo would not be genetically hers because, being post-menopausal, her ovaries would not be producing eggs. It would probably be the product of her male partner and an egg-donating female. The Egg Donor Program of the Los Angeles-based Center for Surrogate Parenting facilitates such transactions. For $6,750, a woman can arrange for a donor's egg to be fertilized with the sperm of her choice and than implanted into her own uterus. And for around $18,000, she can arrange to have the donor carry the baby to term. Egg donors are twenty-one to thirty-six-year-old mothers who receive $2,000 for each donation, a far cry from the $50 fee Cryobank sperm donors receive. But then it's much more time-consuming to donate eggs than it is to donate sperm.

Couldn't a bio-time-clock woman with a little foresight arrange to freeze some of her eggs until her financial and social life stabilized? Unfortunately, human eggs do not freeze well. Other than sperm, the only baby-producing entity that does freeze is a one- to two-day-old embryo. Since embryos can be safely frozen for up to ten years, and women have been known to carry a baby to term at the age of fifty-four, time can ultimately be bought!

Clients of Pasadena's Huntington Reproductive Center can spend $1,650 to arrange for some embryos to be produced and frozen at the clinic's facilities. The Center will only freeze embryos with a custodian (no orphan embryos allowed!). After the first cool year, a $10-dollar-per-month storage fee is charged. Egg donors are generally unwilling to donate to a single woman, so if your eggs are still functional, perhaps your best bet would be to secure a sperm donation, arrange for some embryos to be produced and then put them in the deep freeze. Then you can breathe a sigh of relief that you've done everything technologically possible to someday (within the next ten years) give birth to a baby that's genetically yours.

Even if the unforeseen happened and you, our high-tech bio-time-clock woman, did arrange for some embryos to be made from your eggs and the perfect stud sperm donor, and for some reason your uterus had to be removed, you'd have recourse. An embryo in its amniotic sac is like a parasite. To grow, it simply needs to attach itself to a hospitable blood supply. A woman who had no idea that she was pregnant underwent a hysterectomy, and the young embryo floated off into her abdominal cavity and safely grew to term. Under experimental conditions, men have had embryos implanted into their abdomens and carried them for up to six months. And despite lawsuits, women will probably continue to rent their wombs to embryos whose genetic parents are willing to pay between $25,000–$40,000.

ARE FATHERS REALLY NECESSARY?

As my exploration caused me to think of men as sperm producers rather than fathers, I felt tempted to ask the underlying and perhaps disconcerting question, "Do children really need fathers?" When the only defense one of my students could offer was, "Who will the child send a card to on Fathers Day?" I sensed that in some circles fathering exists only as a commercial scheme to sell more greeting cards!

Looking deep into prerecorded history, we find little reason to believe that the earliest humans recognized fathers. We do know that for the last 70 million years, that is, ever since there were primates, mothers have been important. The most essential human bond is the mother-infant bond. Even today, there are some cultures that do not recognize the connection between sex and reproduction. Often, the most important male in a young child's life is the mother's brother (maternal uncle).

Early human groups may have been socially similar to baboons, whose females form life-long relationships with each other and care for the young together, while the adult males transfer from one troop to another. There might also have been some parity with orangutans, where apart from sexual contact, males and females do not socialize. Mother-child pairs form the basic orangutan social unit.

Human males traditionally have gone off for long hunts or to war, while females have stayed home to care for the young. Perhaps only in recent history was fatherhood invented, once males made the connection between sex and reproduction and tracked it in order to insure a biological connection to their heirs. Restricting the sexual activity of their female partners and endearing those females to them by providing food and protection could insure that biological connection.

Nonetheless, the culture of fathering is perhaps still in its infancy. Today's men's movement encourages men to father each other, making up in part for inadequate childhood and adolescent fathering. Men are told that if they were fathered better, they'd know their roles with women. Those who attend Justin Sterling's Men's Weekends learn that women can be wives and lovers, but should not be made into friends. Participants are advised to build deep friendship bonds strictly with other men.

If women need men only to provision their nests, perhaps women who can do this themselves don't really need men at all. Science-fiction fantasies loomed as I imagined colonies of women who provided for each other to raise their children. Gender-screened sperm would be frozen and dispensed as needed. If by accident a male was conceived, he would be quickly aborted. Since sperm might not freeze forever, a small breeding farm of males would be maintained. Each day, they would be "milked" for their offerings. Those who refused to cooperate would be hooked up to an electroejaculator for quick and sure compliance.

Girls are said to need fathers to learn how to emotionally relate to men. But in a world where there were only males on the stud farm, then a whole other social-learning configuration would be devised.

A FEW MORE POSSIBILITIES

Back in the real world of 1990s bio-time-clock women, there are several more possibilities. A woman who wants to mother can become a big sister, a scout leader, or volunteer to work with children at church, school, or at a day-care center. She can be a stepmother, an active aunt, or a special person in the lives of her neighbors' and friends' children. Finally, she can move into a house where children are already in place and parent them.

She can also adopt a child. While it's much more difficult for single people to secure an adoption than married couples, increased numbers of foreign and handicapped adoptions reveal that with persistence, just about anything is possible. In the past, adoption records were sealed for eternity and/or destroyed, but today places like the Independent Adoption Center in Pleasant Hill, Calif., enable open adoptions. Here, expectant mothers meet with adoptive parents well before the child's birth. Ongoing social relations are fostered, enabling the child to know where he or she came from.

Despite our culture's disparagement of women who have children on their own and the limited public money available to such children, every bio-time-clock woman who seriously wants children and doesn't have a husband can find a way. She can put together a contract with a like-minded co-parent, secure sperm and become a single mother by choice, buy into an array of high-tech options that could extend her childbearing years, or parent other mothers' children. If the preceding legal and medical procedures seem just this side of exhausting, you might be desperate enough to look for an actual husband. The next chapter provides advice to avoid being taken by many of today's alluring strategies to tie the marriage knot.

Chapter 5

TYING-THE-KNOT STRATEGIES THAT UNRAVEL

❦❦❦

A radio station in Los Angeles invites its nightly teens and twenties audience to call in love song dedications. The dedications evoke a love that is simple, blind, and perfect. Listeners passionately report, "He's great, he's all I've ever wanted." . . . "She's so cute and so sweet, I know that I'll love her forever." . . . "From the moment our eyes met, we both knew that we were made for each other."

After listening to an hour of mushy requests, I found myself wondering why it's so hard for many single adults to find perfect love. How did we get to be so picky, distant and difficult? Why aren't we inspired by all that simple stuff? Why have we fallen prey to the current plethora of "how-to-get-married" strategies?

I met Donna, a bright, fairly rigid, high-tech instruments saleswoman, four years ago. Her relentless search for a husband inspired many of the "what's-wrong-with-this-picture" questions that ultimately led to my writing this book. Now forty-three, she's spent the last ten years doing everything she could to meet a special partner. She's purchased dozens of self-help books, attended hundreds of singles workshops, lectures and mixers, placed and answered personal ads, dyed the gray out of her hair, lied about her age and attempted to recapture her femininity by acting more passive and receptive than she actually felt.

Recently, she collapsed into the extra-long leather couch in the living room of her rent-controlled Santa Monica apartment and faced the grim truth: with her earning power alone, she'd never be able to own a picket-fenced dream house, nor a town house, nor even a garden-variety condo. To afford anything in today's real estate market, she'd need a partner. Seeing no one even gleaming in the distance, she withdrew her $20,000 in savings and took a six-week vacation to Malaysia.

Donna's quirky desperation intrigued me. Here was a woman who could certainly support herself—even saving $20,000 in a not-too-lucrative career—who had engaged in just about every conceivable "how-to-get-married" strategy and basically crashed.

Like Donna, you've probably tried some combination of the five basic "how-to-meet-a-great-guy-and-get-him-to-marry-you" strategies:

1. Play the numbers game (date several men at once and/or pursue a variety of avenues to meet someone)

2. Change your body (through diets, corrective surgery, make-up, hair treatments, dressing sexily)

3. Use courtship manipulation strategies (play hard to get, don't act desperate, mirror his behavior and speech patterns)

4. Become financially (and ideally, emotionally) self-sufficient—pay your own bills, have your own career, buy your own place, raise your own kids, etc. (Or: reduce your feelings of desperation so that you don't need a husband for all of those traditional reasons women have needed men)

5. Become a New Traditionalist—a '50s-style receptive/passive woman traditional men like to take care of

Trying one or several of these strategies will certainly net you male attention, if not marriage, but none of them will build an honest relationship, good communication, spiritual/emotional closeness or honest sexual expression. If you were to follow these strategies without listening to your heart, you might snare a man of means who is attracted to what you've gotten your body to look like, who feels comfortable with your gestures because they look just like his, who plays "new masculine" in tandem with your "new feminine," but who may not ever be able to really be himself with you. Think about it! If you begin a relationship through manipulation, it can be even more difficult to build an honest, trusting and enduring connection.

In exposing these "tying-the-knot strategies that unravel," I'm in no way saying that the courtship dance is a dangerous game we should no longer play. But first we need to acknowledge why we play courtship games—that is, to feel unique and special to our partners.

If you've decided to try to tie your knot, the best I can advise is to avoid strategies that you can't live by, realize the limitations in the strategies you pick, and be honest . . . but not so honest that you can't be romantic, too!

THE NUMBERS GAME

Singles experts frequently advise the lovelorn to expand their circle of dating partners. In other words, you might have to kiss many frogs before a prince (or princess) arrives.

The current wisdom is that first impressions may be deceiving, and that to make a better choice, you need to be a "comparison shopper." However, numbers game players frequently burn out, hibernate, and conclude that there are "no good women" or "no good men." The truth is that marriage is not as necessary as it used to be, which means that many are free to be very picky.

There are basically two ways to play the numbers game: One is to date several people at the same time (keeping your options open), and the other is to make yourself available to meeting possible partners through a variety of means.

In the beginning, many people find the numbers game exhilarating, going to singles dances or mixers and meeting many possible dates. There's nothing like feeling popular after you've been lonely or isolated. Running a personals ad can create a sense of abundance few women will otherwise experience, with many women's ads yielding upwards of sixty responses.

The numbers game does work, especially for people who have never played it before, but it tends not to work very well for people who play it a lot. People who don't usually attend singles mixers/events can profit from attending one or two. However, the more events you attend, the more ads you run and/or answer, the more video dates you attempt, the less effective all of this will be. Why? Because you'll get too picky for your own good. And you'll find yourself rejecting and/or being rejected by equally picky people.

Four years ago, Jill, thirty-five, a then newly-divorced commercial artist, placed a personals ad. When she sorted through her stack of returns, her most hopeful respondent was Larry, an attractive, well-traveled, friendly but low-keyed business consultant. She called him, loved the way he sounded over the phone, and they immediately made plans to meet for dinner. The dinner went beautifully, and feeling already like they were meant for each other, they shared tender kisses in the parking lot and readily made plans to meet again. Their next meeting, over a scrumptious candlelight dinner, led to warm love-making in Larry's bed. But despite their initial attraction, neither was inspired enough to make plans to get together again.

Despite his apparent readiness to meet a woman he might marry, Larry spent the next four years attempting relationships that did not get off the ground. Committed as ever to meeting a totally "right" and compatible person, he diligently followed the personals.

Meanwhile, in an effort to get out of a difficult and confining relationship, and remembering the attention and fun she'd had the last time she placed a personals ad, Jill tried one of the new phone ads. (Here, callers hear an advertiser's voice and respond by electronic voice-mail.) One voice immediately caught Jill's attention. She contacted him, and they agreed to meet that afternoon. Arriving at the designated spot, Jill gazed into the face of a stranger who for some reason seemed a little familiar. Fifteen seconds into the date, she realized the man who so readily agreed to meet his fantasy of Ms. Right was none other than Larry!

After four years, both Jill and Larry were still searching for the perfect (or perhaps by this point semi-perfect) partner. While they still found each other likable and physically attractive, Jill and Larry had to admit, again, that this wasn't "it." Each felt a little foolish for not remembering the other, and uncomfortably exposed in their perhaps interminable search for a thoroughly compatible partner.

HOW I SUCCUMBED TO THE NUMBERS GAME

When I first became single, my main interest was to quickly connect with a nice guy who could fill all of the vacancies my last partner left. I tended to meet one man at a time in informal settings like coffee houses, film screenings, and friends' parties. If I liked a man well enough to date him four or five times, I wanted to get involved. Each of these men rejected me because I wasn't enough of who they were really looking for. Coming out of a seven-year relationship where we were committed to working things out, I was baffled over being dropped for such innocuous reasons.

I was hearing two messages—that I was too ready to commit, and that I had no standards, that I wasn't selective enough. I began to believe that to get into a really great relationship, I'd have to get both pickier and more emotionally independent.

The only way I could appear emotionally independent was to spread my "neediness" around. Rather than having one partner that I told all of my secrets to, I developed a whole stable of sub-intimates. Some were the men who had rejected me but still wanted to be friends, others were men I was trying to get involved with, some were friends who had partners, and some were women who were also looking for partners. During a typical "needy spell," I'd call ten people in a row to tell various versions of the same problem or story. I'd stack my week with different sub-intimates I'd meet for lunch, movies, or hikes. If my basic list of ten got thin, I'd add some extras—I didn't want to be too needy or burdensome on anyone.

Next, I became pickier. Rather than just meeting men in casual, informal ways, I entered the organized singles culture. I went on singles hikes, attended singles parties, and placed and answered personals ads. The sheer quantity of men who wanted me to consider them caused me to create an increasingly steep list of criteria. My first list was fairly minimal:

1. Non-smoker; limited drinker
2. Has some source of income
3. Has a place of residence
4. Has a car (if I wasn't living in Los Angeles, this wouldn't have been on the list)

About ninety-five percent of the men I met fit these criteria, so I added more:

5. Politically progressive
6. In his 30s–40s
7. Likes cats
8. Physically active (perhaps works out!)

9. Eats a healthy diet

About seventy percent of the men met these criteria, and so I launched into a level of requirements that almost no one could completely fill:

10. Has a full head of hair with no or minimal gray
11. Physically excellent
12. Emotionally expressive and available
13. Creative (writer, social scientist, filmmaker) with flexible schedule
14. Childless, but wants children
15. Sexually attractive and compatible
16. Playful and engaging
17. Financially secure
18. Relates well with parents and exes.

After meeting with about twenty men who all failed in some if not most of these areas, I felt horribly misguided. I was becoming miserably picky. Rather than expanding my choices, I had made my requirements so selective that no one was going to be good enough for me.

List makers sometimes fail to consider that satisfying relationships often occur between people whose qualities and characteristics are complementary, rather than similar or matching. Since there are myriad ways any given person could be complemented, a wish list would then be ultimately useless.

As for me, I somehow I met my match in Don, who fit some, but certainly not all of my criteria. I was tired of being so picky, bottomed out on unavailable men, and was ready to cuddle up to someone who made me feel understood. Did dating more than a hundred guys over the last several years and creating an extensive wish list assure me that Don was definitely prince material? No way. As long as he or I had stronger needs to be single and/or feared being too controlled or too understood by anyone, we'd continue building longer and longer lists of what our princes or princesses had to look and be like.

Veteran players of the numbers game tend to find themselves cycling through three states: Numbers (dating lots of people, marking time until they find someone they really like), obsession (hopelessly hooked on someone who is not as available as they would like them to be) and depression (because their last obsession didn't work out and the thought of playing the numbers game again makes them feel physically ill).

Should you play the numbers game? Yes, but realize its limitations. Despite the inherent benefits of expanding your pool of possible choices, unfortunately you can reach a point of diminishing returns. If you meet an acceptable, if not delightful, person and you still want to keep looking, you, too, have let the numbers game get the best of you. Having more choices doesn't necessarily assure that you will make the best choice. Dating one nice person at a time met through friends, parties, and activities you truly like ought to be plenty.

CHANGING YOUR BODY

Humans all over the world engage in rituals and practices to beautify their bodies. What concerns me are those women (and men) who believe they need to dramatically transform their bodies in order to inspire someone else to love them. No longer do just a few quirky actresses and members of the royal elite submit to plastic surgery, liposuction and diets, but now growing numbers of single people use such methods. At any given time, twenty percent of the U.S. population is trying to lose weight.

Gary, forty-one, a recently divorced physician, is one such person. Upon entering the singles market, he found that his excess thirty pounds caused him endless grief. Despite his desire to be loved for who he is and not for what he looks like, he decided that his extra pounds were keeping him from making it to first base. In an effort to remarry, he started a rigorous training regimen to lose what the security of marriage had allowed him to gain.

Janine, thirty-two, a shy secretary, enrolled in a widely advertised diet plan to lose the fifty pounds she felt were keeping her from attracting a marriageable man. In eight months, she lost forty-seven pounds and looked great. The problem for her was that her brain had not readjusted. She still felt fat, still acted fat, and her social life had not improved one iota. Janine soon discovered that when she lost weight, her self-image did not necessarily skyrocket.

Dieters typically forgo the innate pleasures of food for the promised pleasures of a more attractive body. No wonder successful dieters like Janine do not necessarily bring love into their lives. If you equate food with passion, it can be a living contradiction to deny yourself food for, say, four months and then afterwards be able to easily attract and accept social and sexual pleasures from others.

Connie, thirty-three, an attractive psychotherapist, knows the other side of Janine's dilemma. Her weight fluctuates between 115 and 150 pounds, and she, too, suffers from the emotional isolation of weight loss. She finds that when she's dieting, she needs much more attention—a kind of substitute for the food that she's not eating. Yet the emotionally restrictive experience of dieting keeps her from being her usual warm, engaging self. Sadly, when she isn't 115 pounds, few men are interested in getting to know her better. Charming and friendly at 140, she bemoans the opportunities she believes she had the last time she weighed 115.

For some women, added pounds can serve as protection against being treated like a sex object. Women who have never been overweight learn as teenagers how to play off men's sexual advances. They enjoy the charge of being attractive and desirable, and confidently ward off what they don't want. Later in life they may sincerely miss those whistles, snickers and sexy jeers. Women who lose weight and are suddenly barraged by male sexual attention may find it disgusting, if not terrifying. Regaining their lost weight may be their only strategy for being treated as a person again. No wonder dieters whose personal lives don't improve don't stay thin for long.

Cara, thirty-six, an attractive hair stylist, has never had a weight problem, but recently she decided that she'd had enough of her small-busted figure. She did what some women only dream of—she had her breasts enlarged. While certainly eye-catching, her new breasts don't particularly match the rest of her body. Nonetheless, she reports that it's a "real charge" when a guy lifts up her blouse for the first time—his look is so different from the "nothing look" she used to get. But the breast enlargement probably hasn't enabled her to meet a more marriageable man. At best it's broken down one level of male physical resistance. Underneath, she's still Cara.

The popularity of breast augmentation today seems to reveal a growing desire to appear more feminine. But at $2,000 per breast, the procedure may prove to be one of the ultimate quick-fix remedies. Why is the procedure so popular now? Perhaps the promise of fulfillment through our careers or the forging of our own professional identity just hasn't happened or hasn't made the difference we wanted it to make. This then may lead to second thoughts about the promise of fulfillment through enhanced femininity.

In today's picky singles marketplace men, too, have felt the pressure to enhance their physical appearances. The "baldness repair" industry has grown by leaps and bounds. While there is nothing medically deficient in a balding man, the pharmaceutical industry and plastic surgeons have positioned themselves to make substantial profits from naturally balding men who want a youthful, sexy appearance.

The Mind/Body Split

Though my body is thin, I often feel like a chubby, clunky, young woman with unkempt hair, thick glasses and baggy clothes. That was me in my early twenties. Then, I was determined to be taken seriously for my brain—and terrified to take a free ride by manipulating my body. Over the last several years, I've felt safe enough to become thin, sexy and seductive. What's been satisfying is finding that with my new look, I can maintain my integrity. Still, there are few female role models for being beautiful, sexy and respectable. While I'm confident enough to display and enhance my body, I still feel guarded about being sexy and seductive. That's only for fun—I still want my professional achievements to result from my mental abilities.

Western medicine also separates our minds from our bodies. It presupposes our illnesses have a specific date of onset and to get better, we must cure our physical symptoms. Meanwhile, tribal healers link our emotional states to our physical bodies. They focus on curing the out-of-balance person as a whole. Perhaps this message of healing the person rather than fixing the physical body has important implications for those of us who believe that if we looked better, then our personal relationships would be better.

Courtship Manipulation Strategies

All cultures have a courtship dance: a set of behaviors that each sex practices to engage attention and interest from the opposite sex. Several of today's singles experts have extracted and enhanced these folklores and produced a set of precise rules and strategies. These fall under:

1. Putting your best foot forward.

2. Disguising who you really are.

3. Manipulating your desired partner's perception of you.

4. Creating a "feeling" of comfort between you and your desired partner.

5. Producing ultimatums.

Generally, these behaviors are practiced just long enough to achieve that desired result, commitment. Then (presumably) upon this bedrock of "white lies," you can try to be real. Some of the most widely read courtship manipulators are Margaret Kent (*How to Marry the Man of Your Choice*) and Tracy Cabot (*How to Make a Man Fall in Love With You*). Kent's suggestions include how to dress, how to sound better educated than you are, and what to feed him. Instructions on dress focus on form-fitting, but not necessarily sexy or high-style, clothes. For the woman who wants to sound sophisticated, she suggests eliminating certain colloquial phrases as well as providing tips for improving one's vocabulary. Potential husbands are to be fed nurturing, domestic foods like milk and cookies.

Kent implores women who want to marry to put aside having fun on their dates and instead pursue discussions of life, death, morals, money, and the future. Readers are instructed to offer a palatable mix of praise and criticism to endear themselves to a man. Finally, she lays out specific instructions for when and how to ask for a commitment (after six months of dating and if his response is not affirmative, move on quickly to someone new).

Tracy Cabot promotes a set of strategies designed to make a desired partner feel comfortable, connected and, of course, ready to commit. Based loosely on neurolinguistic programming, her method encourages readers to *mirror* their partners' dress (wear his colors, styles; dress as if you were already a couple) and their gestures (use your hands/face/body the way he uses his). Instructions are offered for assessing whether his orientation is visual, auditory, or kinesthetic. You then talk to him accordingly, using phrases like "I see what you mean," "I hear what you're saying," or "I know what you're feeling." As you become more intimate with your desired partner, you are to *anchor* him; that is, to touch him in such a way that you indelibly imprint him—so that he associates all of that closeness just with you.

According to Cabot, she used these techniques to lure her husband into marriage. But is she still mirroring all of his quirky gestures and wearing compatible clothes? No way! She openly admits that once married, she quickly reconfigured the relationship, telling him to get rid of those tasteless clothes and stop using his hands and face in such an unbecoming way. While she's apparently having her cake and eating it too, it's likely he's feeling awfully manipulated, if not outright angry.

Professionals like Tracy Cabot and Margaret Kent may be highly skilled in the subtle arts of courtship manipulation, but what happens when a desperate amateur tries? Sally, thirty-two, an aerobics instructor, grew tired of "all of this dating and never getting a commitment," and carried around Margaret Kent's list of suggested topics for first and second date conversations. Did they work? She confessed that her dates were a bit stunned by how many questions she asked. An exasperated breath later, she complained, "They just don't seem to want to marry as much as I do! . . . They're just not taking it as seriously as I am!"

Uninitiated men who attempt to date a courtship manipulator can be thoroughly baffled. Jeff, thirty-four, dated Linda, thirty-six, a courtship manipulator, for about six weeks and determined that, "despite all of her questions and her almost fanatic desire to do everything right, I had no idea who she was or whether we'd be good together."

Despite her underlying sincerity, Linda, like Sally, was so anxious to get into a relationship with a fail-safe marriage guarantee that she couldn't be herself. That anxiety may be the problem for anyone who tries too hard to speed up the courtship dance.

Even beyond maneuvering someone into "falling in love" and going through the motions of making a commitment, courtship manipulation strategies are disgracefully vacant in the areas of honestly expressing personal feelings, getting along with someone who turns out to not be as perfect as the originally evoked fantasy, and staying in love after the fireworks.

INTERNAL BEHAVIORAL CHANGES

The following strategies involve changing not just your activities, but also your attitude. To practice these, you would need to change both the way you experience the world as well as your entire style of living.

Pay Your Own Bills/Take Charge Of Your Own Life

Some women's self-help books and magazine articles have proposed that women need to take care of their own finances, careers, and self-esteem before getting involved with men. Women's dependencies are seen as overwhelming to male-female relationships; women are best off independently shaping their own lives and accepting that, as Sonya Friedman's book asserts, *Men Are Just Desserts.* Similarly oriented books that encourage women to be their own persons and stop depending on men include *The Cinderella Complex* and *Why Am I Nothing Without a Man?* This strategy disregards our human need for intimacy, whether or not we've worked it all out. It fails to address every woman's and man's need to be held, to cry, to be responded to, to be cared for and to be loved. Women and men who keep these needs on hold for long periods of time may be dying a slow death.

Contrary to these theories of self-reliance, relationships can be appropriate arenas for humans to work out their dependency needs. A relationship can allow us to address our otherwise buried needs to be dependent. All of us have unmet emotional needs from childhood. Successful adult relationships team up partners who have complementary and/or compatible sets of childhood neuroses. Two fully emotionally independent people would have no need to be involved with each other or anyone else.

These days, many people go into therapy to learn to build "boundaries," to develop a social strategy to contain their dependency needs. Humans, in fact, have a long history of interdependence. For centuries, we have lived in the company of others—in tribes, villages, and in extended families. Only during the last 100 years have we seen our extended families displaced by nuclear families. The pressure on nuclear families to fill the social, emotional and financial needs that our extended families once filled is a powerful factor in today's high divorce rate. Now, the remnants of family culture are being replaced by a more reliable and rewarding culture of individual achievement. Meanwhile, we see therapists to learn to live in what can only be called an aberrant world. What used to be regarded as a normal human need for love and attention is now treated by our highly individualistic culture as a weakness!

In fact, many women who pay their own bills and live comfortably don't happen to be married. An astonishing eighty-five percent of female executives are unmarried, contrasting sharply with the eighty-seven percent of male executives who have stay-at-home wives. Of the women with doctoral degrees I interviewed, several admitted that even as they entered graduate school, they sensed that this pursuit would probably reduce their chances of getting married. Feminist/writer Barbara Ehrenreich notes that while women are now free to marry men who are shorter, poorer, and younger than themselves, few of them do. Even women who don't need the money are unlikely to marry men who make less money than they do.

Elaine, forty-two, a gregarious and successful real estate agent, admits that she will casually date men whose incomes are lower than hers, but contends that it wouldn't be good for his ego or their future relationship for her to be the principal provider. Even Natasha, twenty-two, a beautiful and engaging college student, is reluctant to get involved with men whose career aspirations are less than hers. While she admits she enjoys the company of her grocery clerk boyfriend, she's worried that as her career advances, he'll become threatened by her success and try to sabotage their relationship. Meanwhile, she finds the guys with high career aspirations to be much less decent, less loving and trustworthy than her sweet grocery clerk.

By giving up the traditional ways women measure success in men, Karen, thirty-five, a freelance journalist, recently stepped into a whole new level of personal and relationship satisfaction. During the six years she had been involved with her last partner, a successful attorney, she had let her career sit on a low simmer. Subconsciously, she sensed that if there were things that she needed or wanted, he would be there to help.

Her new boyfriend, Jack, simply lives by the seat of his pants. He travels to exotic places as often as possible, cooks low-cost meals at home and takes her to plays and concerts by winning free tickets over the radio. Because of Jack's financial instability, for the first time, Karen has taken her career seriously. She's published several major articles and just signed a contract to write her first book. As for the communication aspect of being involved with her new boyfriend, she remarks, "I've never felt so peaceful, so happy and so understood!"

Karen's satisfying connection to Jack certainly challenges the fallaciousness of the "pay-your-own-bills/take-charge-of-your-own-life" (and then pursue a relationship) strategy.

THE NEW TRADITIONALISM

Several years ago Donna read *Smart Women: Foolish Choices* and Toni Grant's *Being a Woman*. She became convinced that what she had been doing was all wrong—that her directness, assertiveness and independence were scaring away the men who could commit. She began to revise herself along "New Traditionalist" or "retro-feminist" lines.

New Traditionalists say women need to make themselves more feminine and receptive by revising their aggressive feminist–inspired personas to attract men who will marry them for keeps. Followers are offered instructions for appropriating traditional values through relearning (or recreating) dating codes and behaviors, including flirting, acting mysterious, reducing career ambitions, and focusing on the nurturing, loving and spiritual aspects of being a woman.

Psychologist Dr. Pat Allen offers two weekly lectures to an overflow, upscale West Los Angeles crowd on "how to be a woman" and "how to be a man." Allen refers to Jung's masculine and feminine personality archetypes to illustrate how feminism created chaos for today's men and women. She contends that feminism is responsible for a generation of tough Amazon women who cannot attract men and a generation of men too effeminate and wimpy to attract women. Men, she claims, want women to be feminine again, while women want men to be cool, decisive and self-assured.

To deprogram women of feminism's damage, Allen's female audience dutifully raise their hands in unison to pledge:

On my honor, I promise that I will never verbally ask men for more, better, or different time, sex, love or affection. I realize that to attract a man I must taste, sound, smell and look good, and be available and appreciative.

The most powerful woman, Allen claims, is passive. She attracts. A woman needs to present herself as sensuous and sexual; she shouldn't bulldoze a man with her brains.

If a woman happens to have brains and has gotten quite comfortable in using them, Allen advises that she close her mouth and focus all of that brainpower through her eyes into flirtation:

Eye him unabashedly for five seconds. Smile. Wait for him to walk across to you and speak. Do not speak first. . . .

According to Allen, a "woman on the remake" should stay silent for at least a couple of months—enough time to let the guy feel "old-time masculine" and in charge.

If a man doesn't know how to play masculine (because feminism robbed him of his training, too), he can be trained to appear strong, secure, decisive and confident.

In time, Donna met Peter, a forty-eight-year-old high school teacher, at a singles event and did the best she could to follow the New Traditionalist rules. For the first four months, she never placed calls to him; she only allowed herself to return his calls. She did all she could to bury her troublesome aggressive Amazon persona and remake herself into being truly "feminine." She resisted his attempts to be sexual with her until he offered her an exclusive, long-term commitment. Then she regularly faked orgasms and barely uttered a word of what she really thought of him in bed. She withheld her real feelings, her anger and her confusion.

As might be expected, about a year into the relationship Donna and Peter both started feeling depressed. They were going through the motions of being "boyfriend" and "girlfriend" by going out on the weekends, taking trips together and buying each other gifts, while their real emotions remained hidden. Peter lost his job and wanted Donna's support. Rather than being sympathetic, she backed off. She wanted him to be confident and financially generous—he wanted her to love him and not his image. Rapidly, the stereotypes they'd been using disintegrated. The insecure parts of him came out, and her selfish, isolating persona emerged. They couldn't handle who the other one really was and they eventually broke up.

The New-Traditionalist rules worked, in that they got Donna and Peter into a relationship. But because Donna and Peter held on to those rules so rigidly, they were prevented from either initially facing their basic incompatibility, or building an honest, durable relationship.

For women who came of age during the '60s and '70s, the New Traditionalism demands a profound attitudinal shift. Feminism gave women permission to focus on independent achievement, but many have concluded that this wasn't enough. The last several years have produced what might be called "post-feminist fallout." Women in their thirties and forties whose careers were advanced by feminism are now frustrated by their lack of husbands, lack of children and/or lack of money to comfortably raise their children.

Did feminism really sell these women short? Perhaps, but the story is much more complex than that. As men and women in the '60s and '70s built relationships that delighted in a sexual chemistry and were grounded in shared interests and common beliefs, relationships that simply traded sex or intimacy for commitment or money diminished. What wasn't foreseen was the daily work that these new relationships required.

Countless women expected their careers to be more personally fulfilling and/or lucrative than they have turned out to be. Despite the increased professionalism of women workers, the majority of women work for wages and not for prestige or personal fulfillment. With record numbers of baby boomers glutting the work force, competition for the best jobs is fierce. As a result, some women have decided to direct their energies to marrying the money they can't make themselves, conceding that they have not quite become the men they want to marry.

Single women in their thirties and forties who don't have successful careers may face a dual dilemma. Do they figure out a way to make a decent living, or do they figure out a way to marry the money they haven't yet made? Sandra, thirty-four, whose graduate liberal arts education netted a depressing array of low-paying clerical and waitress jobs, is one such woman. Recently, she returned to school, hoping to become financially stable. The process has been gut-wrenching. Saddled with unpaid loans from graduate school and an uninsured car that's constantly on the verge of breaking down, she has no health plan to pay off bills from her frequent stress-related illnesses. While she wants to be able to pay her own bills (and that's why she's pursuing this second career), her overwhelming poverty makes her believe that she can only afford to date "men of means."

Last year, Sandra became involved with Frank, a depressed/emotionally repressed man who took her out to the best restaurants, bought her all the clothes she desired and gave her large sums of money to help her meet her expenses. While Frank was more than willing to finance the relationship (she'd even charge her gifts to him on his credit cards), she'd complain bitterly about his inability to engage her emotionally.

If Sandra had a viable career and could pay her own bills, would she be able to afford a lower income/emotionally available man? Perhaps. Meanwhile, Terry, thirty-six, a teacher's aide, whose husband was killed in an auto accident, so desperately needs a husband's income to raise her two kids that concerns about emotional compatibility seem irrelevant. No, she can't make the time to study something more lucrative—she needs a wealthy husband now!

Sexual Repression And The New Traditionalism In Our Lives

One of the cornerstones of the New Traditionalism is a return to women's sexual repression. While fear of AIDS has caused both men and women to take more time to decide who they'll be intimate with (and in turn take on fewer lovers), many women are using any number of ideologies to renew their virginity.

There are women like Carmen, thirty-eight, a member of a sex and love addicts support group, who has been celibate for the last eight years because she hasn't met anyone she feels is worth a committed relationship. Then there is Lorena, thirty-one, who found that every time she had sex with a man where there was no relationship or promise of one, she'd have a herpes outbreak. In an effort to improve her health, she has vowed to have sex only with men with whom she shares an emotional and loving connection. Brenda, twenty-eight, stopped having sex three years ago, when she joined an Evangelical church. The church taught her that sex was too sacred to practice outside of marriage. When she attempted to practice her new ideology on the guy she was then dating, he quickly disappeared. She reports that now she's much happier, with work in the church apparently filling her needs for recognition and community.

Janet, thirty-four, had a brief stint as a model before she was hired on as a Playboy bunny. In her twenties, at the height of her physical beauty, she was admired, well-paid and very secure. Now, she can no longer command the bucks to fund the lifestyle to which she has become accustomed. Though it was second nature for Janet to trade her beauty for money, she realizes as her beauty fades, she may have to go for the big trade: withhold sex for a commitment. While it's not quite in her line of work, she claims, she is desperate enough to try.

Cara also believes that withholding sex until a serious commitment is established will more readily lead her to the relationship of her dreams. She attends Pat Allen's lectures for inspiration and dates frequently. Whenever a relationship doesn't work out, her explanation is either the guy wasn't enough of a "gentleman," or she blew it by getting carried away and having sex before a solid commitment was established.

I wondered how this alluring woman, who tells me how much she likes sex, really follows these rules. She doesn't. Or rather, she has different rules for different guys. Men who present themselves as gentlemen experience her as a commitment-conscious lady, while she readily jumped into a torrid affair with Bill, whom she didn't find stylish enough to be her husband. Her behavior made her a lot more believable to me, though I can't say it gives New Traditionalism a very good name!

There are a couple of problems with New Traditionalism. First, the "Jungian" archetypes that Pat Allen and Toni Grant refer to distort Jung's teachings. To Jung, a full person is someone who fully integrates both their male and female aspects. While feminism may have overcompensated for the lack of Amazon or animus (the Jungian term for the masculine aspect of females) in many '50s women, killing her off by being an airheaded flirt produces an equally out-of-balance persona.

Another Jungian psychologist, Jean Shinoda Bolen, draws from the Greek goddesses and uncovers not two, but seven female archetypes. Three thousand years ago, a woman or man could worship many distinct and complementary gods and goddesses, rather than a single supreme being. Women could integrate aspects of Athena (intellect), Aphrodite (sex, love, procreation), Hera (marriage), Demeter (mothering), Persephone (dependence, compliance, passivity), Artemis (independence, achievement), and Hestia (patience, wholeness). Through Bolen's *Goddesses in Everywoman*, you can identify your feminine parts in one if not several goddess archetypes and move well beyond traditional sex role stereotyping.

WILL THE NEW TRADITIONALISM RESURRECT THE '50S?

The New Traditionalism suggests that we recreate the sex role stereotypes of the '50s because they seemed to work so well forty years ago. However, remember, it was those "happy" suburban housewives who, frustrated by living through others, launched the women's movement. As *Ms.* magazine editor Letty Pogrebin noted in *Los Angeles* magazine, "You can't pretend to be Little Miss Pleasure Giver forever. You're going to get very angry eventually and start asking, `What about me?' "

One reason the '50s are remembered so fondly is because of the post-war economic boom. There was plenty of low-cost housing, and one man's salary could adequately support a household. In the early '50s, only nineteen percent of the work force was female, as compared to the current figure of sixty percent, reflecting the fact that women's work has become an economic necessity rather than an option.

Perhaps we can learn from women who have never expected men to be their sole providers. Many of the young African-American men and women I interviewed in Watts proposed their ideal relationships as one in which there was an underlying feeling of give and take, and both the man and the woman worked. Men could not imagine marrying a woman who did not work. Meanwhile, women who had always taken personal financial responsibility for their and their children's lives, looked forward to the social, emotional and financial input of a live-at-home husband.

Although we now live in a world in which women don't need to marry for social identity or economic support, the pressures to be good communicators, best friends and satisfying partners in every aspect of marriage ultimately make us vulnerable to the magic of formulas. Many of us have fallen prey to manipulative strategies that promise, at best, single-dimensional ends. While these strategies may deliver what we think we want (marriage), we remain socially isolated. This isolation often causes us to make overwhelming social, emotional, financial and sexual demands on our partners, too often destroying the fragile relationships we so desperately need.

The problem isn't the strategies per se. They are simply a manifestation of the fragmentation of family and community in our post-modern society. Our need for love, recognition and community is perhaps why we resort to strategies and why, despite our best intentions, many of our attempts at relationship and at marriage are not successful. In the next chapter, we'll explore why it's much more than the short-sightedness of dating strategies that keep men from marrying women.

Chapter 6

MEN WHO MAY NEVER MARRY

❧•✔

W omen who would like to marry are most concerned with the men who may never marry them. Despite fix-yourself psychology books that tell women they love too much, pick the wrong men, and don't look, behave, or talk the way a marriage-minded woman should, we're going to look at the men. In as realistic and non-judgmental a way as possible, we're going to look at what has kept the male half of the equation from marrying.

If this book were titled *Men Who May Never Marry*, readers might have thought it was about egocentric playboys, with a chapter or two about some troubled wimps and jerks who just can't seem to get to first base. It also would have been remaindered within six months of publication, because our culture doesn't emphasize marriage as being necessary for the identity of adult men.

Since men traditionally propose marriage, perhaps single men should shoulder the responsibility for their own increasing ranks. According to a 1987 Census Bureau study, there are larger numbers of never-married men than never-married women in every age group up to sixty-five. Because the services that marriage traditionally satisfied can now be bought in the form of housekeepers, babysitters, fast-food, take-out, microwaveable convenience foods, restaurants, call girls, surrogate mothers, and someday male pregnancy and artificial wombs, the desirability of marriage for men may well be diminishing.

Traditionally, a man displayed maturity by marrying. He was no longer simply interested in furthering his own achievements, but saw himself as a sort of benefactor for his wife and future children. They would carry on his name and benefit from his reputation and bread-winning abilities.

Men place much value on love as a reason to marry (author Warren Farrell contends that the primary reason men now commit to women is for love), but they are also keenly aware of the restrictions and implications of marriage. Bachelor parties frequently feature opportunities for one last fling before a man surrenders to being committed, faithful, restricted, obligated and shackled.

WHY MEN MARRY

Despite its connotation of entrapment, marriage may represent the necessary display of maturity, or show social and career success for men. A married man is regarded as a more serious and committed professional in many corporate settings. Men who come from stable, loving families may marry to recreate the positive feelings they experienced growing up. Or men may marry to do better for their wives and children than their fathers did for them.

Men may find that marriage gives their lives purpose and meaning. They may also live longer and more happily. In a baboon troop, the central provider/protector alpha-males live longer, while the peripheral, adolescent males may die fighting predators or each other. Despite the even number of male and female births, the overall gender ratio in a baboon troop is typically one male to four females. Sociobiologically, it may be healthier for males, primate or human, to be responsible for females and offspring.

MEN WHO SAY THEY WANT TO MARRY BUT WON'T

Dr. Charles A. Waehler, a psychologist at the University of Akron in Ohio, conducted a study of white heterosexual never-married bachelors between forty and fifty years old. According to Waehler, "If men have not married by forty, they are likely to remain single for the rest of their lives."

While a portion of men in his study were happy with themselves and their lives, many of them still expected to marry. Some of these men were socially isolated—they seldom interacted with others and had a limited sense of themselves. Poor communicators, they might be regarded as "Men Who May Never Bond." They might fantasize about their attractiveness and desirability without knowing how women really perceive them.

Others in Waehler's group might take a woman's polite response to a conversational question as a sincere interest in getting involved. Without actually spending any time with the woman, they might claim they were in love with her. Still others operated in private realms, giving peculiar responses to anxiety-provoking events. They would make offensive remarks to a woman without any sense that she might feel hurt.

While Dr. Waehler's findings made basic sense, I sensed major omissions in his story. First, in the last twenty years, living with a lover has become so socially acceptable that many men now past forty have had years of committed relationships without the legal documentation of marriage. These men have been live-in fathers of their and other men's children, and have been full and loving members of their households. In contrast, the bachelors Waehler described seemed quite out of touch, if not outright deviant. As a psychologist, Dr. Waehler's interest in this subject likely came about through counseling troubled patients. Rather than considering the social, cultural, and economic factors that have caused men not to marry, he limited his focus to men whose self-perceptions are out of focus. Having interviewed and/or interacted with countless "Men Who May Never Marry," I've found the story to be much more interesting and much more complex.

MEN WHO NEVER WANTED TO MARRY

Barry, fifty-two, loves the companionship of women, but has never wanted to marry. He and men like him (and I've known many) enjoy meeting new women, romancing them, and at times getting fairly involved. Nonetheless, the notion of marriage—of a legally sanctioned, full-time, live-in commitment to one woman—has never been of interest to them.

When he was growing up in New York City, Barry preferred spending time by himself rather than with his family. When his parents and siblings went out on Sundays, he'd find excuses to spend the day alone. Family activities were uncomfortable for him then and later, when he grew up, they remained unattractive. As a young man in the early '60s, he moved to Greenwich Village, where he had a rich and exciting social life totally separated from people who valued or aspired to marriage. Living in Santa Monica in the '90s, Barry feels compelled to defend himself:

> I never wanted to marry and still see no value in marriage. I never wanted children. They would be disruptive and make a mess of things. I like having adult conversations with adults. And I very much like women. I love hot, juicy sex. Having a woman's body caress every part of me can be absolutely exquisite. I love getting all dressed up for a date and taking a woman someplace special and having a fabulous time, but I'd rather be gagged with a box of those smelly lubricated condoms than to ever, ever marry!

Barry rarely gets all the sex he fantasizes about having. Angry at the games marriage-anxious L.A. women play, he frequently sabotages potential partnerships by sexualizing them well before the woman is interested or ready. Then, he blames the women:

> It's like we're on different planets. They think they can persuade me to marry them. You wouldn't believe the offers they've made. It's like I'm their last hope for entertainment and for intimacy. What happened to all the independent, adventurous women I knew when I was twenty-three?

Barry's tongue-in-cheek humor and wise worldliness have produced numerous unwanted marriage offers for him, but women have never, ever thrown themselves at Craig, thirty-eight. Thanks to a rigorous workout schedule and near-daily tennis games, Craig looks great. Interpersonally, he's a bit of a disaster. He doesn't understand why women back off when they see he cannot function on an emotional level. Recently he took a workshop on "power dating," where he was given a set of strategies so he might do better with women.

As a result, Craig approaches women as a clinical challenge, figuring out what to say to produce appropriate responses. (In his course, he was told to schedule the first date on a weekday night at a Mexican restaurant. The reasoning: Since it's an inexpensive place, the woman won't feel uncomfortably wowed, and if the mood strikes, the music would be lighthearted and fun to dance to.) While he now knows how to get through the first date and perhaps has gotten dating phrases, gestures, and moves down to a science, marriage remains uninteresting.

When Craig was twenty-eight, he elected to have a vasectomy, out of terror of becoming a father. The only child of emotionally frigid military parents, Craig wouldn't want to wish his kind of painful childhood on anyone. Meanwhile, he feels frustrated by women who expect a level of intimacy that he has no experience in generating. He and men like him may be a sad statement on what centuries of repressive socialization have done to the emotional accessibility of many American men.

Craig and Barry may openly abhor marriage, but there are men such as Steven, forty, who feel so integrated and complete within themselves that they have little need for a female life partner. Steven works round the clock as an avant-garde photographer and songwriter. When he's not addressing his emotional journey through the arts, he meditates. While he enjoys women and reports that he does well with them, he doesn't walk around with a gap for a woman to fill. In his mind, he doesn't need to be in a relationship to be whole. In fact, he looks down on men who do:

I've fashioned a life that's absorbing; I'm not like the kind of guy that lies to and manipulates women to get them to have sex with me. I don't need women in that way. I'm the relationship. There's no other that would make me feel any more happy or any more complete.

MEN AND REMARRIAGE

Men are most likely to remarry because they need to. They generally remarry sooner and are more interested in remarrying than women. Single fathers of young children are prime candidates, as are men whose only avenue to intimacy is women. Men whose experience of marriage was loving and nurturing usually want more. Today's country music is filled with painful tales of men who lost the woman who showed them how to savor life. On their own, they whine and moan about getting a sweet woman back in their arms again.

Widowed men remarry because they are often uncomfortable being alone: There is a nurturing deficit in their lives. These men are generally one-on-one relaters whose model for social, emotional, and sexual intimacy is the couple. For them, a social life is something that a wife provides and a husband receives. For a man to build one for himself is unfathomable. Bert, widowed after thirty years of marriage, clearly wants to marry again. And there's no reason he won't. He's loyal, trustworthy, and a good provider. Moreover, his social skills are so limited that a marriage-minded woman can be assured that he'd never run around on her.

Divorced men remarry because they can afford to. For middle-income men supporting children from previous marriages, the added expense of a new family may be fearsome. But those at the bottom of the financial spectrum may have no trouble easing themselves into a relationship with a woman whose house is paid for and material needs are covered.

Men may also remarry to prove to themselves that they can do better than they did the last time. Perhaps they hold fond memories of their parents' relationship and want the same for themselves. When Kirk's first marriage didn't work out, within a year he bounced back and got into one that did. He desperately wanted a family. Kirk's memories of growing up were so loving and positive that he craved to be like the father he grew up with:

I would have felt like such a failure if I couldn't get into a good marriage. Being single was bearable, but marriage and a family were really essential for being the man I wanted to be.

In some ways Kirk wanted the framework of married life much more than any woman in particular. His priorities focused on a woman who wanted to be a mother (of his future children) much more than a woman who would be a perfect hot-sex/soul-mate/lover.

Since there is a ten-to-one ratio of single women to single men over sixty, men like Frank, seventy-two, report having had dozens of opportunities to remarry. Frank, however, isn't interested. He'd rather keep his own hours and see women on his terms rather than theirs:

I'm really not interested in the burden or the obligation of a full-time, live-in relationship. I've loved and lost enough over the last fifty-odd years that I'm just not motivated to put myself through all of that again. While I enjoy friendships with several women—I'm not interested in having them lead to more. It would be too much of a drain on me. Right now, I'm finally getting to know myself. . . .

Jeff, forty-nine, hasn't bothered to file for divorce for a marriage that ended twenty years ago. By being legally married, he's kept himself socially insulated from marrying again. When his girlfriend of two years pressured him to file for divorce so they could marry, ambivalence surged:

I suddenly realized why I'd never gotten divorced. After that last time, I had no interest in ever again being married. I didn't want a woman or the state expecting certain things from me—I didn't want to be labeled or to be controlled. Marriage as an institution may have made sense to my parents and people like them, but for me it was cumbersome, preposterous, and had nothing to do with what matters.

A Brief History Of Men And Marriage

Men's ambivalence about marriage is certainly reflected in what marriageable men have done in earlier times. Economics, social expectations, and political realities have all influenced men's decisions to marry. Men have typically married when they could afford to. At the turn of the last century, following the first boom of the industrial revolution, our country suffered a severe depression. Then, a full forty-six percent of American adults were single. Many men simply could not afford to marry. They courted their sweethearts for years, hoping to eventually amass enough money to afford the obligations and responsibilities of marriage.

In Colonial America, financial expectations for men approaching marriage were again quite different. During this period, husbands, wives, aunts, uncles, cousins, and children worked together in cottage-based enterprises. A man wasn't expected to be a provider all on his own; rather, he and his family worked together to make a living.

During the industrial revolution, marriage-business partnerships went out of favor in America. The "traditional family" where the father goes to work to support mother and kids at home became a norm among the middle classes from 1860 to 1920. The wives of successful industrialists came to believe that it was improper for them to work—that their place was in the home. In fact, the first wave of post-industrial revolution divorces were initiated by women whose chief comlaint was their husbands' inability to be good providers.

After the Great Depression and World War II brought record numbers of women to the workplace, the economic boom of the '50s temporarily caused the "traditional family" to come back into style. The prosperity of the post-war '50s permitted a record number of middle-class American men to marry. Heavy pressure was placed on women to relinquish their wartime "Rosie the Riveter" jobs to make room for the returning male vets. With low interest rates and GI bill loans, those vets and the women who married them became the most subsidized generation to ever marry in America.

Marriages in the '50s typically offered men little intimacy and emotional connection. Men became slaves, not only to corporate life, but also to being the sole financial providers for their families. The American male entrepreneurial spirit was for the most part relegated to improving homes and repairing cars.

A virulent seed of the male marriage rebellion was planted in 1953 when *Playboy* hit the newsstands, anesthetizing the pain of men trapped by the blandness and endless financial responsibility of married life. *Playboy* challenged the notion that men should have to pay for sex within marriage by offering up a monthly supply of apparently willing, seamlessly sexy women. In effect, it encouraged its readers to reclaim indoor life by resisting marriage while still enjoying female sexual companionship. According to *Playboy*, a man didn't have to be a husband to be a man. Ultimately, social historian Barbara Ehrenreich concludes in *The Hearts of Men: American Dreams and the Flight From Commitment*, the actual *Playboy* message was not eroticism, but escape from the bondage of breadwinning.

Eventually the "Breadwinner Ethic" broke down. A whole new set of status symbols emerged as American playboys pursued attractive young centerfold-types, hated wives, questioned alimony, and ditched gold-diggers. Rather than financing family life, playboys preferred to direct their earnings to Porsches, classy pads, and classy girlfriends.

Male rebellion intensified further in the '50s with the beatniks, who rejected not just marriage, but work too. Beat poets such as Allen Ginsberg, Michael McClure, Neal Cassady, and Jack Kerouac wrote and took to the road. They rarely, if ever, married; at best they lived off women. According to Barbara Ehrenreich, the beats' "madness to live" largely disparaged women, whose demands for responsibility were were, "at worst, irritating and more often just uninteresting compared to the ecstatic possibilities of male adventure."

Adventurous male rebellion continued with the hippies, who also rarely married and avoided straight jobs like the plague. Hippie men aspired to less polarization between themselves and their "old ladies" by growing their hair long and joining in domestic activities, including bread baking and sand-candle making. They focused on community-sized families rather than bringing home the bacon for just their little nuclear family. Everything personal was approached as something that could ultimately carry global political implications. "Family values" per se were an anachronism in their socially (and often sexually) non-monogamous world.

THE SOCIO-ECONOMICS OF MEN AND MARRIAGE TODAY

Men today who were raised in '50s families face a very different set of parameters than their fathers did. While their fathers joined the gray-flannel-suited masses to work at alienating corporations, the sons came of age in the '60s, when young men feverishly followed their dreams to become rock stars, poets, painters, activists, and intellectuals.

Unlike their fathers, these men and their female counterparts went to college in large numbers. Their college romances were with equally competent and entrepreneurial females. Upon graduation, these females willingly supported themselves. They believed they could be anything they wanted to be and pursued careers as art historians, dancers, singers, masseuses, and social scientists. Few females, however, made long-term financial considerations in choosing their careers. Deep down, they presumed they would be scooped up and cared for when it was time for marriage and children.

Many of the men, however, were ill-prepared for such financial demands. By the mid-'80s, the women in their lives began to reject men who only offered sensitivity and creative independence for men with stability and the ability to provide. Today, the women they know with lucrative professional careers have little energy to nurture an ordinary guy's someday-to-be-something business. Rather, they'd prefer he support their professional endeavors.

A slightly younger and a bit less individualistic generation of '80s men forged a new model: the yuppie. They appropriated materialism with a vengeance, selling their souls to corporate America and living in the moment. These men have been drawn into the traditional paradigm of attracting beautiful feminine woman by presenting themselves as success objects. Frustrated by the materialism and emptiness of such exchanges, a growing number of young men have turned to older women for companionship and sexual attention. These exchanges, though rarely approached as life partnerships, meet basic needs without the cold manipulation practiced in the trade of sex for success. (For more on the dynamics between older women and younger men, see Chapter Eight.)

With male-bashing greeting cards and joke books still big-ticket items (*Everything Men Know About Women* is the best-selling blank book ever), men feel challenged to make themselves attractive to today's women. Many men are baffled about what women want. Traditionally, a man paid for a woman he was courting to demonstrate his ability to provide for her in marriage, but paying isn't much of a symbol for providing when a woman's income is such that she can easily pay her own way through life. Despite these realities, some women with substantial personal incomes nonetheless expect men to cover all expenses associated with dating.

Mark, a retired businessman who recently joined the ranks of single Los Angelenos, claims that the women he meets are so self-absorbed that they are unable to fully engage, let alone respect men:

> *Women don't thank you when you take them out. They don't call the next day and let you know they had a good time, that they enjoyed the dinner, etc. They just take, take, take! That's just the way they are. . . .*

While traditional courtship had a built-in logic for traditional people, today it doesn't. We cannot cram ourselves into functionless paradigms and expect to find enduring intimacy and pleasure. When women expect men to be traditionalists when it comes to paying, but then transform themselves into women's emotional and communication equals during every conversation, it's no wonder men have become wary of dating and distrustful of marriage.

WHY MEN HAVE DIFFICULTY WITH WOMEN

Men have difficulty with women because they've been socialized differently. Moreover, their brains are organized differently. Our hunter/gatherer origins explain the differences. Males who were successful hunters could track an animal for days. They'd focus intensely on every footprint, on every sound, and on every fecal dropping. This ability to concentrate so that all energies were focused upon a potential prey was essential to early human survival. While males were out honing in on one thing until they got it, the females back in camp became multi-taskers. They could comfort or suckle a baby while gathering or preparing food and gossiping. There was no particular order for fulfilling these multiple tasks: sometimes they just focused on the baby, other times, they snuggled the baby while gathering nuts, roots, and berries, and other times when all was still, they might have gossiped about this and that with no linear focus.

Modern humans share much in common with early men and women. Our problem is that we don't realize we do. Instead, men get irritated with women for drifting from one conversational topic to another with no regard for solving problems or completing thoughts. And women become frustrated with men who don't appreciate the value of unloading one's day in four-part harmony. When a man hears a woman's report of having been violated, abused, and misunderstood, he wants to help her get even with the perpetrators. It makes no sense to him when all she wants to do is yell, scream, bitch, and moan.

As psychologist John Gray explains in *Men Are From Mars, Women Are From Venus*, women's brains have more linkages between the right and left corpus colosum, allowing them to easily address many things at once, while men, in turn, go into caves. When a man is in his cave, he doesn't hear anything. He's just focused on the task at hand, and he's doing everything he can to get it done. When a woman attempts to unload the dramas and traumas of her day with a man in his cave, she'd be better off going spelunking without a flashlight.

From the moment John Gray explained his cave analogy, a light clicked on for me. I recalled the utter frustration I'd feel when I'd walk into the house to report a full day's dramas and traumas, only to find my boyfriend so absorbed in some project that he'd barely acknowledge me. I thought his behavior was extremely selfish and rude and vowed never to get involved with a man who behaved this way again. If I had only known that just about all men do this once the high-attention courtship phase subsides, I might have weathered that (and future) relationships' "secondary cycles" better.

Sociolinguist Debra Tannen says in *You Just Don't Understand: Women and Men in Conversation* that dialogue between men and women can be likened to cross-cultural communication: "Women speak and hear a language of connection and intimacy, while men speak and hear a language of status and independence. . . . Instead of different dialects, it has been said they speak different genderlects."

For women, the point of conversation is to build a rapport. There is much pleasure in having the person listening to you get what you are saying. That feeling of deep understanding is of core importance to women. According to Tannen, women converse to establish connections, negotiate relationships, and to match experiences.

For men, however, the point of conversing is to preserve independence and negotiate (or maintain) their status in the social hierarchy. They demonstrate this by displaying their joke and story-telling abilities, their astute insights, and by one-upping everyone else by interrupting, raising their voices, and speaking with the utmost conviction they can muster. With such different conversational goals, it's no wonder that men and women may only make matters worse if the ways of talking were the cause of the trouble to begin with.

What men and women each consider problematical in a relationship may also differ dramatically. One difference, notes Los Angeles psychologist Herb Goldberg in *What Men Really Want*, is that men look for objective, logical remedies to fix relationship problems. Rather than examining deeply embedded patterns, which often reveal why an experience keeps getting repeated, men are more likely to try to quick-fix their "mistakes." This scenario is especially likely in matters of sexual performance. Men are more likely to purchase some contraption that will keep them virile for hours than to speak in a heartfelt way to their partner. While a heart-to-heart talk might not immediately fix a flaccid penis, the effect of such a talk is much more likely to create the kind of intimacy women most hope for when they have sex. Nonetheless, many men, despite assurances, don't feel better unless the manifestation of the problem, the flaccid penis, is repaired. While they are more than willing to acknowledge the psycho-emotional origin of their "problem," they most want to be able to perform like a true-blue stud. Exploring the architecture of the dynamic that caused the "problem" is seen as a waste of time.

Men and women also use very different maps in the arenas of sex and intimacy. While most women are quite comfortable sharing deep intimacies with non-sexual friends, to men, being intimate usually connotes being sexual. Some men are only able to function sexually when they disassociate from emotional intimacy. "In the worst cases," according to psychologist Alan Gross, "sex becomes so incompatible with emotional closeness that it actually seems to pre-empt intimacy." With men's overarching focus on goals, the point of having sex becomes orgasm. This performance can, in turn, become the full basis of men's sexual self-esteem. Moreover, the sharing and emotional intimacy that women seek can easily run counter to achieving this singular male goal.

Anxieties may also arise when a woman rejects a man's monolithic world view. Because many men believe that they can teach women their version of life's objective truths, they'll readily accuse an independent-minded woman of being recalcitrant, naive, and ignorant. When an economic realist/scientist such as Gary, fifty-one, encounters a "magic lady," such as his last girlfriend, a believer in crop circles, witchcraft, metaphysics and UFOs, all hell may break loose. And it did, as Gary reports:

After two years of tiptoeing around her conviction that she'd had regular contact with aliens from the Pleiades and contending with her making our home a "sugar-free zone," I realized that our belief systems would never converge. There's no way I could see myself ever giving up my respect for quantum physics, species evolution, and natural selection to believe that each of my body scars of unknown origin could be evidence that I, too, had been abducted by aliens!

While Gary's case seems quite bizarre, nonetheless, it illustrates a very common dynamic that can be troubling to a man whose data-based, linear, absolutist system is dismissed by a woman whose thought process is based on intuition, a respect for spirits, and hormonally triggered emotions. Similarly, when a woman contrives to seduce a man into being closer to her, it's likely he'll be quite angered when he realizes she never respected his version of reality.

THE REAL STORY BEHIND MEN'S FEAR OF COMMITMENT

Women sometimes point fingers at men for being incapable of commitment, but commitment-shy women often subconsciously get involved with unavailable men because it is still more socially acceptable to be a jilted woman than it is to be a woman who may not be interested in marriage. Commitment-anxious women may either reconcile themselves to their lives as they are—that they prefer the men in their lives to be not particularly available—or they may see through to the other side and connect with a more fully embraceable man.

Many men are, however, afraid—afraid of losing their money, their time, and their wild male spirits. While bachelors in the '50s were disparaged for shirking manly responsibilities, by the '80s bachelorhood was touted as the more masculine alternative. Men registered higher on the wealth and power scale when they invested in their projects, funded themselves, and treated themselves to expensive toys. This culture of individual achievement, rather than intimacy, family, or relationship, prevails as the yardstick for assessing well-being.

Scared of being thrown off course, men have even approached

attorneys to draft waiver agreements for the purpose of one-night stands. Phil, one such man, explains:

I've put everything I've got into my businesses, my cars, and my house. I wouldn't want some bombshell I might meet one night to think she could get to it. I'm not scared of intimacy or anything like that. . . . I just don't want one of those palimony suits to creep up on me. . . .

Phil may not understand emotional intimacy, but he's very clear about what's his to keep and what's his to consider sharing.

Men's movement pioneer and male/female communications specialist Warren Farrell contends that a man's fear of commitment largely reflects a fear of becoming financially responsible. A man who commits gives up his primary fantasy of access to lots of attractive, (presumably) available women. Our culture enforces this fantasy through sex in advertising and best-selling men's magazines like *Playboy* and *Penthouse*.

Farrell attests that men and women have very different primary fantasies. With the best-selling women's magazine *Better Homes and Gardens*, women's primary fantasy would well be characterized as a dream house with a flower garden surrounded by a white picket fence complete with a loving husband and great kids. When a man marries, he gives up his primary fantasy of access to as many beautiful women as he desires. When a woman marries, she attains her primary fantasy of a committed relationship to one man who provides, or has the potential to provide, economic security.

Once married, Farrell reminds us, many women stop working or reduce their work hours to care for children, which in turn raises the financial pressure on their husbands to intensify work. When couples marry, a man's salary tends to go up, while a woman's tends to go down. Marriage's implicit pressures for males to both be faithful as well as to provide for others make commitment a major hurdle in our financially and sexually turbulent culture.

MEN, MONEY, AND WOMEN

Men with unresolved issues about intimacy with women often live out financial and career dramas that keep women at a distance. These include involving themselves in yet-to-be-lucrative enterprises, practicing workaholism, pursuing career interests that typically don't pay well, and subsisting at low-income jobs. Of the many men I spoke with who engage in these practices, nearly all of them were keenly aware of what they were doing and its incumbent impact on their romantic lives. Often they were reeling from relationships with women whose earning abilities, financial styles, and life dreams conflicted with theirs. Their requirements for future intimacies with women always began with wanting the woman to accept them for who they are and not what they might eventually earn.

Money is a major issue for Stan, a forty-three-year-old junior high substitute teacher who has yet to achieve his dream of fathering children in a white-picket-fenced household. The son of Holocaust survivors who raised him with a poverty consciousness, he's had a hard time approaching life as a financial winner. In his last serious relationship, he and his girlfriend had major conflicts about money. He'd work slow and steady and save as much as he could, while she would produce relatively large amounts as a freelance designer and then spend them quickly. Their financial styles were so different he never felt he could trust her. Stan does feel, however, that if he were to meet the right woman, a woman he could trust, he could earn more money:

I believe a woman could inspire me to earn more. I'd start a business. Working now as a substitute teacher covers my expenses. I don't need more money than that. I guess on my own, I don't believe in myself enough to make more money. What would I be earning it for? I'm fine the way I am.

While Stan says he'll figure out how to earn more money if the right woman comes along, Garth, twenty-seven, is outright obstinate in his refusal to change his finances to impress a woman. He recently took stock of his life and concluded that rather than working in sales, he really wants to finish college, go to graduate school, and get a doctorate in Swedish literature. Asked if he thinks his choice will limit his attractiveness to women, he answers:

Honestly, I don't care. I need to be true to myself. I wasn't put on this earth to sell—while it's kept me in nice cars and financed my condo, I can't live that way anymore. If a woman can't accept me for what I love, I can't expect to love her.

Brian, forty-four, faces the other end of the dilemma. He's earned millions as a telecommunications entrepreneur and as a result, attracts zillions of women. His concern is whether the women love him or love the security and material things his wealth has afforded. When an especially beautiful woman he was about to make love to proclaimed she'd like to do it with him in all seven bathrooms of his three-story home, he freaked:

> *She wasn't caring about me; she was just in love with my house. She was probably fantasizing about quitting her job and moving in full time. There was no way she cared about getting to know me—she just wanted to swim in my pool and play with my toys.*

Men who could be on the road to success, like Gary, thirty-three, a screenwriter, and Michael, forty-five, a restaurant owner, often have trouble bringing women into their lives. Gary gets by as an office temp when he's not writing his someday-to-be-a-blockbuster screenplay. Gary confides that if Ms. Right suddenly appeared, he'd get a "real job." His independent creative spirit hopes she stays away at least until he secures a solid option.

Michael's girlfriend left him because he wanted her to continue working as his 80-hour-a-week partner in his yet-to-be-profitable restaurant. The restaurant—while his entrepreneurial dream—became her emotional nightmare. While they spent countless hours together, it was for a dream she had long since lost interest in. The more she worked to please him (read: to connect with him), the angrier she got over the intimacy deficit in her life.

These men, and millions like them, are finding themselves caught in a creativity/success/love warp. They believe if they can only continue to follow their creative, entrepreneurial endeavors, financial success will follow, and with that, they'll be able to attract love from the most desirable women.

Men have begun to look at commitment as a lose–lose proposition. A man who does not earn much won't attract the woman of his dreams, while a man who does will spend most of his time working to support his woman and will have little time to enjoy her.

Psychologist Herb Goldberg contends that men have a blind spot when they believe that women will automatically love them for performing and achieving. If men pay, earn, or produce, and a woman doesn't immediately love them in return, they feel taken. They blindly believe that the more successful they are, the more their partner will happily bask in the glory of their achievements. When the very behaviors that bring them social and financial status (competing, performing, looking out for number one) cause alienation between themselves and a woman, women become pure trouble.

Since drive, ambition, wealth and power are still the ways that both men and women define male success, workaholic men easily attract women. While many work-addicted men are not focused on money per se, they get passionately involved in projects that need endless attention. Workaholics may direct their energies to fledgling theater companies, social and political causes, composing, painting, writing, and certainly business building.

Workaholic passion can be very compelling when it's directed towards a woman. Workaholic men romance a new woman with all the energy they might otherwise direct to an inanimate project. Unfortunately, once a work-addicted man pulls in his prey, the passion gets automatically redirected to work. Then, rather than staying up all night listening to her stories and pleasuring her in every conceivable way, these men are up all night with their computers, their thirty-six-line intergalactic telecommunication systems, their forty-eight-track sound mixers, and their oil paints, pastels, acrylics, water colors and charcoal pencils. What happens to the recently won-over woman? She may leave in a hurry (not a bad idea); she may whine and moan about humane schedules for meals, sleep, and play; or she may fall in love with him just the way he is.

Workaholic men are filled with life purpose. With little interest in seeing the bigger picture, they stay devoted as long as there is a challenge. Richard, an artistic director of a fledgling Hollywood theater, openly admits that his theater is his mistress. Weekends when there's a show, he's committed full time; when the theater's dark, he's on a mad scramble to secure rights to another project. When he meets a woman, he pursues her day in and day out, and just about the time she returns an interest in him, he loses interest in her.

Unlike Richard, Chris builds "enduring" relationships with women despite his ninety-hour-a-week commitment to peace-building. When he's not writing op-ed pieces, designing flyers, training younger activists, and reading four newspapers, twelve magazines and an adventure novel or two, he's on the phone recruiting for the next major event. Julia, his former girlfriend of eleven years, enjoyed being associated with a man who was so selflessly dedicated to important causes. Eventually, when she realized that ninety-nine percent of his attentions could never be directed back to her, and all he wanted her to do was rub his computer-induced sore neck and shoulders, and proofread flyers and op-ed pieces, he became history.

Gila, another of Chris' girlfriends, so respected his commitment to peace and justice that she feared she'd destroy his true spirit if she stayed. She wanted to have children and she knew full well that his sub-sistence-level salary would never fund anything more than his share of the rent, gas, and groceries. If she got pregnant, he'd be forced to take some dull civil service job to pay the bills, and his reason for living—his life purpose—would crumble into mindless mainstream mediocrity.

Roy, thirty-one, dove headfirst into the abyss that Chris so much fears. By twenty-eight, he'd been married nine years to his high school sweetheart, opened his own piano store, bought a split-level home and fathered three children. While everything he'd done looked good, he felt like a slave to his business' and family's demands. It seemed that every-one depended so much on him, but no one really cared about him. No one cared about his real happiness; all they cared about was what he could do for them.

Roy dramatically backed out. He divorced, gave his wife the house, liquidated his business and bought a spectacular motorcycle. Now, he is doing everything in his power to not attract another woman who is a "gold digger." He rents a $200/month room in a friend's apartment, takes daring (helmetless) motorbike rides and occasionally tunes pianos to cover his meager expenses. For the most part, he is happy with his new lifestyle. His only regret is that when women find out how little money he has and how little interest he has in earning more, they drop him like a hot potato.

Kristof, forty-five, socializes much more than Roy, but as for serious relationships with women, he doesn't do any better. A once-successful entrepreneur, all of his major businesses crumbled as a result of the reces-sion. Many thousands of dollars in debt, he keeps from going belly-up by hosting paid private parties at his home. While he is thoroughly charming to the many women who pass through his doors, rarely do they ever focus romantic intentions on him. He wisely ascertains:

Losing all the money I had has certainly humbled me. For however many women I attracted then, I'd say the relationships I do have with women these days are more honest. They know I can't make them promises and can't afford to take them out to dinner. It's lonely but it's real.

Men like Kristof and Roy remove themselves from the singles market by becoming "financial isolates." Despite the numbers of women who really don't need a man's financial assistance, nearly all women fall in love in a context. That context is a demonstration of the potential, ability, and drive to provide and to continue providing all the linings of a love-nest. While women date men who are artists, writers, musicians, bikers, piano tuners, and party planners, it's often through visible demonstrations of his success (such as his car or home) or when he exudes a certain confidence about who he is and what he can do that a woman feels turned on enough to consider him seriously as a potential husband. And men who are keenly aware of the steep financial consequences of appearing like husband material may fashion safe livelihoods that can fall flat when it comes to love, commitment, and intimacy.

MEN WHO ARE IN SEARCH OF THEIR SOULMATES

Men searching for soul mates may be quite oblivious to the sex/success object trade. They just want what they want, without any thought of what they have to offer in return. They may want a statuesque blonde with light blue eyes who wears six-inch heels twenty-four hours a day, who is perfectly fulfilled by inspiring him to be all he can be. Ray, forty, wants just such a woman. As he tells his story, he recalls having settled for less. There were overweight women, overworked women, and women who didn't have blonde hair. Having recently joined a video dating service, Ray has renewed his determination to meet only serious contenders.

Ray and men like him focus on "looking for the one," first, because they have the luxury to look and not find. They live in a culture where it's perfectly acceptable for a man to be single. Second, searching may be more interesting than getting, especially if women find them appealing. Men who were quiet and shy in high school, whose emotional and social skills were arrested in adolescence, may spend much of their thirties and forties making up for lost time. With the cocky jocks and superstars out of the picture, suddenly they can play center stage! All the attention keeps them savoring the hunt much more than actually being involved with any living, breathing, reactive female. Finally, there is the male psychology of dedicated effort causing the final conquest to seem very valuable. A woman couldn't just arrive at a man's doorstep and be recognized as "the one." He has to pursue her, she has to seem somewhat unavailable, and eventually she must notice him, pay attention, and then (as a result of his efforts), she can feel like "the one."

While bio-time-clock women have been known to reduce their acceptable partner requirements down to zilch, their male counterparts, having been looking for so long, refuse to settle for anything other than a soul mate. Josh, thirty-eight, a Santa Monica masseur and seeker, has written a poem to the soul mate he has yet to meet. The last part reads:

> *In the bonding of my soul with your soul—I am home, whole and complete. Then for me, there is only to dance the dance of life with you. . . . You call me forth as no other woman can. It is the blending of our beings that empowers me to be and to be great. It is the fragrance of your essence that inspires me to be my best. That is why I choose you over all the rest! . . .*

Having searched long and hard over the last twenty-odd years, Josh doesn't just want a woman to dance life with, he wants her to call him forth, to empower him, to inspire him, and to cause him to be all that he hasn't yet been. It's a tall order to fill, especially with the plethora of self-absorbed career women that pepper his stomping grounds.

Some men's search for "the one" is conditioned heavily by what they didn't find in their last relationship. Vic, forty-one, a San Francisco–based videographer, relates an extensive list of what he would need to know about a woman before he would marry her:

> *I would need to know her family history: Does she have any inheritable genetic characteristics or disorders? Beyond this, she would have to be very healthy and have a strong constitution. She should have no out-of-control eating disorders nor any addictive or compulsive stuff. While I realize that these disorders are reflections of female internalized oppression, ideally I'd like to find a woman who has survived this socialization and/or has worked to liberate herself.*

Beyond Vic's "politically correct realism," many men's notions of perfect are reflections of what mainstream culture celebrates. These socially constructed notions of perfection are often more what men think they ought to want rather than what might actually make them happy, comfortable, and content. Men whose soul-mate search is infused with contemporary cultural ideals might aspire to acquiring a trophy wife, who may be manipulative, narcissistic, and/or not particularly loving.

Bret Lyon, a Los Angeles communication therapist and Jenny Davidow, a hypnotherapist, observe that men who are looking for "the one" don't understand that their description of her is an impossible-to-fill fantasy:

> *This woman does not exist. They will never find her. They may think they have, for a while, but it will end in terrible disappointment. Or, they may know her already, but have chalked her off as not "the one" because there are some problem areas.*

What soul-mate searchers don't realize, according to Lyon and Davidow, is that relationships are a process. You don't just pluck the ripest, biggest, reddest, juiciest strawberry and adoringly parade it around forever. Relationships involve work; they don't just fall out of the sky and happen.

Perfectly matched soul mates don't just collide into each other one day, sense perfect chemistry, and never for a moment have trouble communicating. Our pop culture rarely feeds us realistic love stories filled with the doubts, fears, and grungy anxieties of real relationships. Rather, we are invited to wallow in magical movies like *Sleepless in Seattle*, in which we are led to believe, moments before the end credits roll, that now that Tom Hanks' and Meg Ryan's characters have finally laid eyes on each other, all will be perfect. Men who are uncomfortable expressing vulnerability, conflict, and strong emotions have trouble realizing that even the best of relationships are not always happy, smooth-running love affairs.

Finding a soul mate is possible. It happens, and it can be exquisite. It doesn't usually happen to people who are searching for a soul-mate, but rather to people who have a good sense of themselves, are perceptive about who could be a good partner, and willingly co-create a "soul-mate feeling."

THE REPRODUCTIVE RIGHTS OF MEN WHO MAY NEVER MARRY

Until very recently, the only reproductive right single men had was the right to a vasectomy. Divorced fathers found themselves with the obligation to pay child support; the only way they expressed their unhappiness with the situation was by not paying.

Now men (usually married) are able to hire surrogate mothers to bear their children and increasing numbers of gay male couples are adopting children. Someday male pregnancy will become a medical reality. Because embryos contain a placenta and an umbilical chord, they can function as a self-contained parasite, attaching itself to any available blood supply. An embryo could thus be implanted in a male abdominal cavity. Supplemented with female hormones, the pregnancy could come to term and be delivered by Caesarean section.

While it is unlikely that millions of men will rush out to be become impregnated, awareness of such medical technology may further free men from feeling they need to be married to become fathers. Like the bio-time-clock women who are having babies on their own, male pregnancy technology may afford men the same procreative independence. They might purchase eggs much the way women now purchase sperm, then arrange for embryos to be made using their sperm, drop by a clinic for implantation, and then, after nine months of gestation, have full parental rights over their baby.

While currently the law is largely concerned with a woman's right to choose to keep or terminate a pregnancy, with male pregnancy technology, men's reproductive rights could be expanded. A man might be legally guaranteed equal rights over the disposition of a fetus resulting from his having had sex with a woman. If she chose not to carry the baby to term, he would then have the right to have it implanted in his own abdomen, and then assume full responsibilities for its care and upbringing. She could elect to have no further involvement as if she had chosen to have an abortion, or she could share in parenting responsibilities at any level she chose. While a man could not force a woman to bear a child against her will, she wouldn't be able to force him to be the social/financial father against his will.

Ultimately, the notion of consent and responsibility for unplanned conceptions could be expanded. A woman could no longer trick a man into becoming a father (e.g. by lying about being on the pill) and then take him to court to pay child support because men could openly become fathers on their own. The courts would never again presume that men secretly wanted their unplanned babies because it would be common knowledge that if a man wanted a baby he could have it on his own!

THE WIMPIFICATION OF MEN

Men are still reeling from how feminism inverted and twisted traditional sex roles. Men who softened themselves in response to feminism's critique are frequently regarded as wimps. They acquiesced too completely to women and lost that wild, dangerous, unpredictable spirit that signifies a full-bodied man.

Over the last fifteen years and perhaps more intensely over the last five, men have begun to band together to assess for themselves what's gone wrong. Through various permutations of the still-fledgling men's movement, men are honoring male friendship and having some of their best heartfelt talks with each other. Jack, forty-five, who previous to diving headfirst into "men's culture" confided endlessly in his female friends, now proclaims:

It's the guys on my men's team who are really important. They're the ones who give me the support I need. I don't need women the way I used to. I date women and hope to marry one someday, but now I've come to realize that women cannot be good friends for men.

What Jack and the men on his team have put into practice is a very old archetype. It functioned well in the days when we lived in extended families and men socialized largely with men, while women did the same with each other. No one expected husbands and wives to be best friends; they married largely to create useful social (and sometimes political) linkages, and to reproduce.

Meanwhile, much has transpired, and I'm not convinced that the best we can do is to go back to the past. While it's true that the nuclear family put undue pressure on men and women to meet all their needs through each other, and the sex-role revolution caused us to see the inflexibility in archetypal masculinity and femininity, we can't go back. Men who have accessed their androgynous selves through the feminine arts or perhaps have explored their actual feminine selves through cross-dressing, transgenderism, and even transsexualism may be another sort of harbinger.

Once the men on Jack's team have exhausted the intentional male bonding of retreats to the woods to drum, hunt, and chant and have made up for all the basketball and football they didn't play as adolescents, I believe they'll come to see value in connecting with their female natures. They won't be so absolutist about recovering their maleness and they'll be better able to build community with women. Moreover, once fathering is reclaimed and given full respect, then I believe men can joyously become wise, useful, and playful parents who consciously integrate both the feminine and the masculine.

Beyond the quandaries created by the sex-role spin-around and a fragile national economy, marriage-wary men continue to face several conflicts that won't go away. First, despite the biological imperative for independent male aggression, males who live the longest and healthiest lives do so as a result of becoming emotionally and socially linked into a familial unit. They do best when they're in a mutually nurturing relationship, receiving the kind of care and attention they were raised with while being appreciated both as a lover and a provider.

Second, perhaps as a result of the intense pressure women place on men, not only to provide but to be fully present and emotionally expressive, the culture of individual achievement continues to hold major appeal.

Finally, nuclear family culture has so failed men that their caution about commitment and marriage remains realistic. This caution will be reflected and magnified manyfold in the next chapter's discussion of the unique dramas encountered by women who may never remarry.

Chapter 7

WOMEN WHO MAY NEVER REMARRY

⋰•⋱

alues, economics, and opportunities have so shifted in our culture that divorcing and choosing not to remarry is now widely understood, if not openly acceptable. There is now little stigma placed upon people whose marriages don't work out, but up through the mid-'60s, divorced women were frequently regarded as sexually threatening. They could lure married women's husbands away! By the '70s' divorce wave, such perceived threats diminished as a variety of solutions for intimacy took hold. Many people lived together without remarriage, carried on monogamous relationships while maintaining separate households, or created communal homes.

As noted in Chapter One, human romantic relationships average between four and seven years. These biologically conditioned norms have become so socially acceptable that now those couples who have stayed married for twenty years or more are regarded as aberrant. Their friends wonder, "Are they truly happy? Have they stagnated each other, or is this for real?"

One product of divorce's increased acceptance is a growing number of women who have tried marriage and now may never marry again. They fall into three categories:

1. Women who will remarry.
2. Women who say they would like to remarry, but probably won't.

3. Women who never want to marry again.

This chapter will focus largely on women who fall into the latter two categories, so let's look briefly at what causes women to remarry. As noted in Chapter Six, men are much more likely to remarry and remarry sooner than women because matrimony is often men's only avenue to intimacy. Women, in contrast, are better able to open up emotionally to one another. In gathering stories for this book, I frequently encountered women who would reveal intensely personal details of their lives within minutes of meeting me. It's little wonder that with such facility at intimacy, women have less need to remarry than men.

WOMEN WHO REMARRY

Women often remarry because they enjoy being paired with a man; they're most comfortable living as part of a couple. They think in twos, rather than in ones, or in clusters. Mainstream culture reinforces this thinking by offering a plethora of married and couple activities, options, and discounts.

Several women I spoke to were so ensconced in couples culture that even though they'd been separated from their husbands for years, they tried to behave as if they were still married. Myra, fifty-five, whose husband left her for a much younger woman, fervently believes that once he comes to his senses, he will be back. He now lives abroad and has fathered several children with this "new" woman, but that hasn't phased Myra a bit. She truly has no interest in remarrying. As for finances and community life, she manages just fine on her own. What may enable her to manage so well is her fantasy that she's married to someone who is in love with her. Her state may be similar to that of a Catholic nun who shares such a covenant with God.

Women also remarry for money. Jill, thirty-nine, openly admits that she married her second husband because his income would allow her to stay home with her children and never work again. As she calculates:

I'll be the first to admit that our sex life is nothing to brag about, but having a beautiful home, a full-time housekeeper, and being able to spend as much time as I want to with my children have made remarriage for money the best decision I ever made.

Women who want children seek remarriage with a man they can envision building a proper nest for the future. Jannie, the bio-time-clock massage therapist in Chapter Four, teeters between marching off to the sperm bank and becoming a mother on her own and making a last-ditch effort to try marriage one more time, as long as the contender vows to be a social father/sperm donor/provider:

I really hope Mark, the guy I've been dating, works out. It would be so much easier to have children with a real father, but it's so hard to tell after a couple of dates whether it's going to work. It's horrible having no time to wait! I wish I could just close my eyes and have him be right.

WOMEN WHO NEVER WANT TO MARRY AGAIN

Women who don't need to be married for money, status, or social identity contend they have paid their dues as the number one nurturer, food preparer, mother, and homemaker. They are no longer interested in washing, ironing, cooking for others, cleaning up after others, or sleeping next to someone who continues to snore even after being gently kicked, rolled, and perhaps pounced upon! These women may reap the benefits of a former husband's estate, freely glide about from a comfortable divorce settlement, or they may come into their own power through business. Divorced women who become Hollywood producers and real estate agents often draw from the social, mediation, and home management skills they honed as mothers and wives. For once, these skills prove to be lucrative in their own right.

Elaine, an English-born psychotherapist in her fifties, recalls that when she first married, she gained tremendous fulfillment from assisting her husband and, later, her children. On her honeymoon she remembers washing her husband's socks—this role felt so natural and so right. During the early phases of marriage she assisted him in building his dream business; he made all of the creative and business decisions, while she kept track of the administrative details. She remembers:

I just loved nurturing his dream. He was the star of my life. To make him happy and successful made me happy and successful. If this was true love and true marriage, I loved it and could never get enough of it.

Elaine's blissful spell dissipated as her children grew older and she faced how much she had been living to please others and how little she knew herself. She returned to school and became a professional in her own right. There was a huge disparity between herself as a wife and the woman she could now fathom being as a psychotherapist. While Elaine the assistant could be her husband's wife, Elaine the psychotherapist, with her own office, business plan, and practice, no longer experienced fulfillment as a wife—not just as her husband's wife, but as anybody's wife.

Bonnie, like Elaine, also has no interest in being anybody's wife. At fifty-three, she's a business manager who has weathered two long marriages, raised two daughters plus one stepson, and now truthfully enjoys being single. When questioned about remarriage, she comments:

> *I'm really tired of taking care of other people. That's what marriage was— meeting the needs of my kids, supporting my husband's businesses—it seemed like all of me was spent caring for others. Honestly, super-honestly, I want the rest of my life for myself. I want to spend the money I earn on me and I want to choose every day if and how I'll expend myself on other people. . . .*

Growing numbers of women like Bonnie and Elaine, who spent the majority of their adult years in the service of others, are now, for the first time, truly expanding their professional wings—and nothing is holding them back. Their children are raised, their houses are well-financed, and they have large communities of friends. All the traditional reasons that women have needed marriage no longer apply to them. They may be the closest that women in American society have ever come to being truly independent. Their male counterparts don't understand. These men, often with more status and income than ever before, feel bullied and frustrated by these women's lack of interest in the traditional trade of nurturing and home care for financial maintenance. The men, however, don't understand the spiritual/life force drain once-married women fear they'll experience if they ever again live through others. For them, a comfortable home and spending money is no trade once they're focused on themselves.

MOTHERS WHO DON'T WANT TO MARRY AGAIN

These women's focus shifts from other to self when they know they can't go back. One day Virginia, forty-eight and a mother of two teenage daughters, dramatically walked out. With her daughters in tow, she packed a couple of suitcases and drove to a local battered woman's shelter. When she saw her daughters absorbing the behavior that had caused her to become victim to her husband's battering, she knew there was no turning back. By the time I met Virginia, she was no longer teetering as the object of her husband's rage. Rather, she was working full time and had enrolled in a college program designed for working adults. Her term paper on battered wives was well-researched and emotionally astute, revealing her total change of attitude about men. Once so dependent as to be a victim, she was now unequivocal: She had no use for men as partners, co-parents, nor for any form of social identity or economic support. She was clearer about her sense of purpose on her own.

However many single mothers yearn to find a man to share parenting with, at least as many, if not more, prefer parenting alone. Barbara, thirty-seven, knew Jim less than six weeks before she became pregnant with their daughter, Chelsea. Over the next two years, she struggled to put together a good home life for them all. Jim, however, was on another wavelength. His ideas about what children need differed dramatically from Barbara's. She contended that Chelsea should grow up in a smoke- and drug-free home, but he persisted in indulging in his favorite habits. Angry, she completely withdrew sexually:

> When I couldn't trust him alone with Chelsea, how could I possibly be his lover? How did I know that he wasn't going to be so stoned out of his gourd that she wouldn't be safe? Pretty soon, Chelsea became the person I cared about and protected . . . and the less she and I saw of him, the better everything was.

Veterans of painful marriages like Barbara and Virginia may eventually conclude that intimacy with their children is so absorbing that seeking out a man becomes superfluous. Suddenly, there are no more arguments about parenting styles, no more power plays. Whatever Mom says is law! Thus today, as in the earliest human settlements and in all primate species, the mother-infant bond remains perhaps the strongest family tie.

Women who enjoy the companionship of men but don't need them to father children or buy houses may engage in a lower-stakes trade. Rather than trying to become involved with men who fear being taken advantage of financially, these women take in men who have nothing much to lose.

Abby had always lived in ways that her friends and family would approve of. In her mid-thirties she married Jed, a kind, successful, and worldly businessman. They travelled, adventured, and looked happy to their friends. After several years, Abby reported that she was suffocating and was soon divorced. It wasn't until her early forties that she fell in love again; and this time it was with Jeffrey, a man who was the complete antithesis of Jed. Jeffrey had barely completed high school, didn't work and didn't care to, had no worldly ambitions, no friends, and a life lived mostly in a stoned stupor. With no obligations to anyone but her, Jeffrey tended Abby's every need. He cooked wonderfully and was the best lover she'd ever had. After several years of housing Jeffrey, Abby began to reflect on what had become of her life:

> *My home barely resembles one belonging to the woman I see myself being. The shades are always drawn, it reeks of cigarette smoke, the TV is on constantly, and it's littered with Jeffrey's endless messiness. I know there's been this rebellious part of me that's needed to say "fuck you" to everyone who expected me to conform. . . . But this has gone too far. I've done enough of Abby the rebel.*

Juliet, a social worker in her early fifties, like Abby, also rebelled when she invited Arturo, an attractive Mexican in his twenties, to move into her home. Her youngest son had recently moved out to live with his girlfriend when she met Arturo at a wild bar south of the border. He begged her to sneak him into the U.S. When Arturo first arrived, he helped her with yard work, fixed leaky faucets, and often washed the dishes. What he and Juliet didn't share intellectually and aesthetically, they made up for emotionally and sexually. After a while, Juliet's friends began to wonder what she was getting out of keeping Arturo. He started helping around the house less and drinking beer and watching TV more. Juliet admitted that Arturo was taking advantage of her, but it took her eight years to ask him to leave.

Juliet's friend Carmen also got deeply involved with a man who was far from her equal. Carmen's companion, Frank, was ten years younger than she and still waffling about who he wanted to be when he grew up. He saw himself being a wildly successful author and lecturer known for brilliant insights. While Frank attended every transformational workshop he could afford, he never did manage to think many original thoughts or write any of them down. When they first met, Carmen informed him that her three children were all she wanted, and that her tubes had been tied. Though Frank went through the motions of fathering Carmen's kids, deep down he wanted his own biological children. Frank wanted to be a human equivalent of the trusted and respected protector/provider alpha male mountain gorilla, distinguished by his fantastic silver back. By the time Frank met Carmen, the configuration of her life was such that she had no use for a silverback in her home. While not all male gorillas assert the silverback desire, those who don't rarely attract females into their polygamous "harems." Similarly, because Juliet and Carmen own their homes, and have all the children they want, their lack of need for a provider/protector husband causes them to draw in men that ultimately frustrate them by having so little to offer.

THE VULNERABILITY PARADOX

Women who say they would like to remarry but probably won't are often victims of the vulnerability paradox. These women are so anxious about ever again surrendering to a man that they fashion lives in which they constantly produce and direct their own one-woman shows. They may travel fast and furiously to parties, bars, and dance clubs in search of peak moments. Since these moments don't last long, the women may have an insatiable appetite for more. Their behavior unconsciously insures that they will never marry again. At thirty-eight, with her long, dark mane and sexy gait, Loretta is a pro at luring men in, getting them very interested, and then backing off. Rather than admitting her role in these dramas, she constantly blames the men. By blaming them, she feels righteous in sabotaging their efforts at getting close:

You wouldn't believe the losers I've been meeting! They lie through their teeth about how much money they have and how available they are. How is it that an "available man" is unavailable for a 11:30 p.m. phone call?

If these women aren't seething with anger like Loretta, then perhaps like Colette, thirty-nine, they wallow in a world of fantasy. Vulnerability may be so distasteful to them that they create fantasyships (as opposed to relationships). In these fantasyships, they are able to keep a distance and thus stay safe, keep all of their power, and thus avoid surrendering much of their inner being to anybody else. Their pleasures may come from telling and retelling the enviable stories of their many romantic adventures. As Colette reports:

> I think the best part of all of this is telling my girlfriends all the details! Describing each of the kisses and how perfectly they were delivered—it was like living it again, only better!

Sometimes, as with Colette, the fantasy-laced retelling becomes more satisfying than actually relating to a man. After all, thrills may be much more interesting than being chilled in a relationship. Charise, forty-four, began to understand this phenomenon when she tried to explain why, after being divorced for the last fourteen years, she hasn't remarried:

> I've got to admit that I love the rush of meeting someone new and savoring whatever happens. I love first kisses. I love finding a man who really knows his way around my body. I love hot surprises. For however much I've been saying I want to remarry, I think I really like my roller-coaster life!

Alice, fifty-three, a veteran of the best Beverly Hills plastic surgeons and regular workouts with her personal trainer, came full circle after a life assessment therapy weekend with one of Los Angeles' foremost psychologists, admitting:

> There is no reason in the world why I would want a full-time man in my life! Part-time lovers are great. All a full-time man would do is keep me down. . . .

Alice, with her properties, money, and freedom, may have constructed a fortress around herself. Looking like a very young forty, she attracts an exciting array of playboys and players. When she's had enough, she exercises her freedom to send them on their way.

Like Alice, Maria, a college admissions counselor in her early fifties who has been single for the last twenty-five years, is fully aware of the vulnerability paradox. A Chicana from south Texas, she wants to trust men but doesn't want to give up her hard-won freedom. She earned an advanced college degree when few of her peers did, bought her own home, and created a social life in which she could be constantly center stage. The thought of giving it all up to merge with a man who might temper her wildness is pretty scary. The vulnerability paradox so overwhelms her that she, too, may never marry again.

Unlike Alice and Maria, Tamara, fifty-two, is hoping after several failed marriages to finally get it right. Lacking the money that keeps Alice in her perfectly controlled glass house, and the restrictiveness of Maria's cultural upbringing, she's ready to give vulnerability a try:

> *I want to do the growing I was always too scared to do. I don't want to live out the rest of my life being so angry at men. I want to be able to let go and feel safe. I'm tired of being so guarded and getting involved with such guarded people!*

Every boundary for women like Tamara, and of course Alice and Maria, gets fetishized. Rather than trusting their feelings to assess each man they date for who he is, they create rigid rules and boundaries, such as:

1. It's okay to date, but there can't be sex.
2. It's okay to have sex, but he can't stay over.
3. It's okay for him to stay over, but he can't leave anything.
4. It's okay for him to stay over and keep a toothbrush in the bathroom, but he can't have any closet space!

Tamara struggles to find the inner strength to allow herself to let go but not lose herself, to experience what she hopes will be a blissful surrender/merger of two conscious spirits. Ultimately, her social, professional, and economic independence make this quest simply another growth option rather than a necessity for either happiness or survival.

MAGIC LADIES

Women have always created special worlds that only they understand. These worlds give them a connection to powers larger than themselves . . . and certainly, they believe, larger than the kind of power men wield. The world of these "magic ladies" can feel so encompassing that the world of men and romance may pale in comparison.

Magic ladies greatly value the wisdom of psychics, healers, mind and body readers, and channelers. They may practice spells and rituals in groups to bring each member's desires to fruition. Each shift in their lives is noted as evidence that their powers are at work!

In Berkeley, a group of Hispanic women gathers each month to practice the lore of their Aztec forbears. They recall spirits and sensations that resonate through the psyches of women. While the men's auxiliary may beat drums and dance, the women's connection to mother-earth forces guides their community.

Magic ladies may regard themselves as receivers of God's light. This light, they say, works through them to bring healing to the earth and to themselves. Rather than taking responsibility for what they see or say, they surrender, not to men, but to higher powers. "Light workers" may journey to the "power spots" of the world, such as the pyramids of Egypt, ancient ceremonial centers of the Incas and the Yucatec Mayans, as well as the vortices of Sedona, Ariz., and Santa Fe, N.M. Through chants and rituals, they seek to connect with deep supra-human truths. Toni, who recently returned from one such journey, reports:

> I never before felt so connected to what matters. For the first time in my life, I felt spirit, and it was—I don't know how to say it—it was incredible. It warmed our hearts and made everything good again. All the things that used to bother me about men and relationships just faded away. . . .

In the Pasadena-based Circle of Power, women gather every other week to offer support and express their coming week's desires. The divorced women in the group frequently request new male partners; such desires, however, are rarely realized. One of the founders confirmed my suspicion that the group had, in many ways, superseded its members' needs for relationships with men:

> If our members really wanted new husbands, our powers could certainly make that happen. They still think they should want men, but I think what's really happened is that the loving power we generate together actually satisfies the desire for family, love, and intimacy.

For women whose marriages meant blind submission to a husband's wisdom, tapping into powers generated without men wins hands down.

Women who tune into magic are no longer constrained by the ideology of modern capitalism. Rather than accessing wealth through work, or love through relationships, they create insular matriarchies with their own rules, standards, and language. Suddenly, there is infinite power and each woman believes that by subscribing to rituals, chants, crystals, and perhaps some potions she can generate all the wordly goods she really wants. A woman, once she harnesses the powers available to her, can attract all the wisdom and healing she needs to make her life plentiful. The traditional trade of sexuality and nurture for finances and social identity appears irrelevant in this female-controlled universe.

Travelling in a realm devoid of male linear thinking, magic ladies may frustrate men no end. One such lady prohibited her boyfriend from reading the newspaper and watching television news because, she said, "everything we need to know will come to us." Having the upper hand on "wisdom" that most men consider shaky, magic ladies are relegated all the more to a goddess-rich world of their own making. Moreover, when males peer in to watch the goddesses dance, their interest is rarely just spiritual. Their puerile curiosity merely confirms to the magic ladies that they are light years beyond men's lower chakra (sexual) concerns.

WOMEN WHO HAVE (RE)CLAIMED THEIR SEXUAL POWER

Women who don't need to marry again may come into their own sexually for the first time in their lives. Rather than satisfying their husbands to keep a roof over their heads and food on the table, for once they set the terms. They may court boy toys and then discard them as soon as they become whiny and possessive. They may organize December/May social clubs to find more hard-bodied studs. (These older women/younger men clubs seem to always be founded, controlled, and run by the older women; the men are courted largely as objects for the women's fancy.)

Laida, in a quest for sex, power, and spiritual wholeness, presents herself as what might best be described as a tantric sex goddess. She moves with an other-worldliness that entrances men instantly, while retaining full power. A man who was engaged by her at a party recalls:

While she looked like a woman, she didn't behave like one. She was so focussed on being in control, she never connected with me as a person. I could have been anyone. I was simply a vehicle with which she could perform.

While her performance may have looked pretty amazing, it was, at best, for everyone to watch. I know it wasn't for me.

Laida pleases men on her terms while remaining blithely uninterested in an enduring relationship, but women like Stella embrace a sexuality in which men are neither the object or the subject. No longer feeling the need to please men, their families, or to uphold mainstream cultural sexual standards, they have come out as gay or bisexual.

Stella's marriage was largely a business arrangement. Her husband, Ted, worked hard as a physician while she raised their children and kept the house in order. When Ted wanted more sexually than she was interested in satisfying, they became swingers. While swinging provided Ted with the variety and charge that was missing in his marriage, its openness to female bisexuality unlocked a whole new world for Stella. The swingers' oblivion to sexual bonding repulsed Stella, but she sensed that to keep her marriage, she couldn't tell her husband "no." So she became deeply involved with Jeanne, another married woman. When Stella's husband died, it was clear in her mind that there was no way she would ever marry again. She had no use for another passionless marriage, nor was she interested in spending another minute in what she regarded as the "male-fantasy inspired" swing culture. She did, however, love Jeanne. And while Jeanne remains married, the friendship, passion, and love that sustained Stella through her vacuous marriage is still present today.

Lida's husband completely lacked the stability and commitment Stella found in Ted. He was a fast-talking alcoholic who charmed women almost as fast as he discarded them. Once divorced, she borrowed some money from her parents, found a full-time job, and took responsibility for raising her two children. After her parents passed away and her children left home, there was no one left to please or impress. For the first time in her life, she was free to do what she wanted to do. Blistered by the horrors of her married life and then single motherhood, she had no interest in pursuing intimacy with men. Women, however, were something new. She joined a midlife women's support group more for succor than for romance, though gradually she and another member grew to love each other so much that recently she decided to come out as a lesbian to her children. They were stunned. Suddenly their mother, their bulwark of conventionality, had asserted herself. She no longer cared what they thought. She was just going to do what felt right to her!

Women in their forties, fifties, and sixties who own their own houses, have full professional identities, and are responsible for their own livelihoods may remain emotionally and sexually alone. These women, like Judith, a philosophy professor in her early fifties, contentedly go to professional and social events by themselves. In Los Angeles, it's thoroughly acceptable for a professional woman to attend conferences, film screenings, award ceremonies, and dinner parties on her own. No one expects her to make the pretense of bringing a date. If she's not out fulfilling her own social or professional agenda, then she works in her garden, feeds her cats, and feels a certain relief from the social whirl of people who are still looking.

With little need for what men have traditionally offered women, these once-married women often complain that there are no longer any men they can look up to. In their twenties, their culturally programmed desire to "marry up" was easily satisfied. Now, they fear being controlled and "de-selfed."

OPTIONS BEYOND TRADITIONAL MARRIAGE

Women whose social and emotional appetites cannot be adequately satisfied by an intermittent scattering of professional meetings and activities may build an "extended family of choice." Such families provide their members with everything from trips to the airport, help during an illness, travelling companions, and holiday gatherings to warm hugs and soothing massages.

Claire, who is part of such a family, compares her life now to her life during her ten-year marriage:

> *I now have more close friends, and altogether, share more with them than I was ever able to share with my husband. I have three or four men and at least five women with whom I share all kinds of real personal stuff. When something difficult happens, I can easily call ten people in a row to talk it all through. I love having so many sweeties!*

However close we are to them, the "families" we have created may not seem enough. To accept them, women need to realize that there may never again be someone just around the next corner to scoop them up and marry them, as there was in their twenties. Once this "loss" is reconciled, then marriage can become only one of a panoply of options, and the intimacy paradigm can expand. Then we women (and men) can freely negotiate for what we want. Perhaps we'd be happier in a part-time relationship, with intermittent vacation sex, taking a woman lover, being part of a triad or a group marriage, or calling the shots among a secret array of multiple partners. In the next chapter, "The Sex Lives of Women Who May Never Marry," we'll explore the dramas and passions women experience in satisfying their need for intimacy.

Chapter 8

THE SEX LIVES OF WOMEN WHO MAY NEVER MARRY

••

U nmarried women have realistic and sometimes unique ways to satisfy their sexual appetites. The pressure to find a husband may be so exhausting that they engage in "lower stakes trades" with men who, in their minds, couldn't qualify as husbands.

We should remember that long ago, when all humans were nomadic hunter-gatherers, sexual activity was not linked to reproduction. When a woman became pregnant it was seen as her powers alone (or perhaps those of fertility goddesses) that generated life in her womb. These humans had a oneness with nature; there were no double standards for the expression of male vs. female sexuality.

Once men recognized the power of their role in reproduction (possibly through early efforts in stockbreeding), a double standard emerged. Sexuality became charged with power and with significance. Men began to limit the activities of their female partners to assure proper inheritance to their heirs.

Women's sexuality became regarded as mysterious, complex, diffuse, and dangerous. In an attempt to control female sexuality there have been (and still are) cultures, largely in the African Sudan, that have removed the clitoris in young girls before they even know its value, its power, and its sensitivity. Often grandmothers perpetuate this practice to insure their granddaughters' acceptability to husband/providers. Despite numerous health education efforts, the pivotal conditions that are enabling young girls to keep their clitoris are expanded educational and employment opportunities for women. The more women don't need to be married to live comfortable lives, the less grandmothers clitorectomize their granddaughters.

Western women for whom the right to keep one's clitoris has never been questioned do not easily become comfortable with themselves as sexual beings. Traditional girls are raised to regard their virginity as a prize to be awarded to one husband, and rarely acquire skills in the art of being a responsive and enthusiastic lover.

Parents often make it difficult for their daughters to enjoy, let alone embrace, their sexuality. Janet, twenty-eight, fondly recalls sharing countless secrets with her parents, but eventually she concluded:

I've given up telling my parents anything to do with sex in my life. I've faced that at best they're interested in romance. . . . Their fears for my safety far override any concerns for my sexual pleasure.

Unlike sex education in other world cultures, in the West we focus almost exclusively on safety. We encourage our teenagers to "just say no" by warning them of the dangers of AIDS, pregnancy and rape. In contrast, among the Muria, a tribal group in India, girls and boys from early adolescence until marriage spend each night in a *ghotul*, a dormitory where sensitive and practical sexual learning occurs. By the time young Murias marry, they will have been fully schooled in a wide range of partner-pleasuring techniques as well as having a thorough sense of how their own bodies work.

We Western women have a long history of trading sex for commitment; today, some single women who'd like to marry still use sex as husband bait. Cornelia, a thirty-two-year-old dancer, says that her desire to marry has placed an often unbearable pressure on deciding when to be sexual with a man:

I'd really like to stop trying to get married. All of this trying has really kept me from being all I can be. I keep worrying that I might not be doing it all right . . . and if I don't do things "right," marriage won't happen.

Like Cornelia, a lot of lonely people think they'll continue to be lonely unless they "do it right the next time," whatever "right" is. If there were any sure-fire magic formula, they'd swallow it alive.

THE "RETRO-FEMINIST" BACKLASH

The backlash against feminism in the last ten years resulted in the popularity of "retro-feminist" (or New Traditionalist) dating strategies. One of these, as we discussed in Chapter Five, advises women to withhold intercourse while bartering their sexual attractiveness for a marital commitment. Retro-feminists claim that women with low self-esteem "put out" too soon with men: If they thought more of themselves they wouldn't be such "pushovers." Women who aspire towards these rules and restrictions may then blame their lack of a committed relationship on having "gone all the way" too soon.

The retro-feminists were part of a group of "singles strategists" who claimed to know the answers to questions on "doing it right" in sexual matters. Most popular among these questions were: "Does holding out help build a stronger, more enduring relationship?" And if it does, "How long should one wait?" And, "Is there a window of opportunity in which the waiting is really stalling and that initial spark will fade into ashes?"

Among these strategists, the female experts generally tell women to wait—that sex is good only when it's founded on a solid relationship. And most male experts claim that there isn't any one right time, but warn men against raising expectations for commitment they might not be willing to fulfill.

However, take it from me: I know that some of these women who write advice books don't actually wait—they just advise their readers to! And their readers, determined to get into long-term, marriage-producing relationships, are willing to do everything under the sun to "do things right." Or, like Cara with her torrid-in-the meantime affair with Bill in Chapter Five, they'll readily have sex with men they don't consider candidates for the "real relationship."

Women shouldn't necessarily hold off on sex until they sense relationship potential. According to Paula, who has been in several long-term relationships, withholding sex has little to do with building or not building a relationship. She slept with her husband of nine years the night they met and married him soon after. In her mind:

Getting to know someone includes getting to know them sexually. If sex gets withheld for the right moment, it gets made into this real big deal, with real big-deal expectations. Sex is a process, not a result.

There's probably no connection between when sexual intimacy begins and how long a relationship lasts. Certainly people who wait to have sex are more likely to have more relationships last longer since they'll be "prediscarding" a fair number of potential partners. I've heard countless stories of couples who made love on the first date, moved in with each other soon after, and continue to share the most wonderful relationship. And I've heard about couples that courted for years before actually consummating their love and that worked, too. (Basically, what works is when couples share a common view of the courtship process.)

Women who try to separate their sexual expression from their emotions can get caught. Some of the women I spoke to who were active participants in the sexual revolution remember those times as sexually unpleasant. Holly, thirty-eight, recalls:

> I just did what guys told me to do. I acted like I liked it. Truthfully, when I really think about it . . . all I was trying to do was to get a boyfriend. And I thought if I showed him a good time, he'd come back for more.

Men didn't necessarily come back to Holly for more: not because she wasn't good in bed, but because they tend to experience sex and emotional intimacy oppositely from women. When a man meets a woman he is attracted to, often his first desire is to have sex with her. Once that happens, he will begin to evaluate whether he might like to be in a relationship with her. Before a woman has sex, she tries to assess whether the man is someone she can trust and would like to be in a relationship with. By the time she says "yes," she may feel quite ready to commit.

A man experiences a woman's "yes" as a validation of his masculinity—it establishes (or reconfirms) his identity as a desirable man. Before a woman says "yes," she holds the power to make or break the pending relationship. As soon as a man hears her "yes," he scoops up the power. As long as he is the one who is expected to make the next move (and call her the next day, or in the next two days, or three days, or five days, or whatever it is she believes is the "right" amount of time), he holds "time power."

Women relinquish "sex power" when they judge a man is interested enough to call the next day. But what if he doesn't? Well, he doesn't know anything about "girl time." The moment he kisses her goodbye, "girl time" starts ticking. If he doesn't call by 4 p.m. the following afternoon, adrenaline will start coursing anxiously through her veins. If he doesn't place that call before bedtime that night, he's in deep trouble. She's already begun to remove him from her "this-could-be-the-relationship-I've-always-wanted" fantasy to serious contemplations of "what went wrong" or "maybe he just wants to be friends."

Women don't deal well with the disparity between "girl time" and "guy time." They might try to busy themselves with some useful (or at least time-consuming) project, bitch and moan to as many willing girlfriends as they can locate in the next forty-eight hours (who, ideally, will sympathize but offer no advice), take a sedative, consider suicide, or call him and act as cool and calm as possible.

Because women are socialized to put relationships ahead of just about everything else, they may go into rages over men who don't call (soon enough). Perhaps women should give men contracts with stated requirements for making subsequent contacts before they sleep together. That way she could sue him if he failed to call by 4 p.m. the next day and/or didn't take her out to dinner the following weekend!

Psychologist Dr. Pat Allen, who lectures to thousands of Los Angelenos on relationship strategies, actually advises women to make a contract with the men they agree to be sexual with. The contract is expected to address issues that can be mutually agreed upon: Will this be a one-night stand, occasional casual sex with no possibility of a commitment, or the true-blue, exclusive, ongoing committed relationship?

Dr. Allen's "First-Stage Dating Contracts" haven't gained major popularity among women because they're not very romantic, and a woman wants a man to want to romance her. She wants him to be so impressed that he would naturally call by 4 p.m. on his own. Making agreements ahead of time makes sense as long as no one changes his or her mind. However, many men and some women can think straight only after they've consummated the encounter they thought they wanted so much.

Beyond researching newfangled strategies for women who will ultimately do what they damn well please, I went to the deep South, where I presumed there was a whole tradition of the Southern belle and her dapper gentleman beau. Like Scarlet O'Hara, who adeptly got everything she wanted from Rhett Butler in *Gone With the Wind*, these women didn't have to read about male-female strategies in books, I thought. They, I believed, had had the opportunity to absorb them innately. Rita, thirty-three, who lives in southern Mississippi, sees relationship strategies as quaint and unfamiliar. She reports being pretty straightforward with the men in her life. Gail Gibbons, an Austin-based psychotherapist, sees such strategies largely as an unobtainable archetype. They represent the out-look of women from a period her clients have little skill or interest in replicating. From what I could uncover, Southern women, unlike the L.A. singles strategists, clearly have no upper hand on courtship manipulation.

OTHER-FOCUSED VS. SELF-FOCUSED LOVERS

Women who trade sex for marriage may become other-focused lovers. They make love to please their husbands rather than to satisfy themselves. They willingly satisfy his requests, demands, and desires. They are their lover's lover. Even when a lover says he is there for her pleasure, an other-focused lover will have little sense of what she wants. She fakes moans, groans, and orgasms to make him feel powerful and that he's given her pleasure.

Many women with an appetite for sex, but little interest in marriage, are the knee-jerk opposite of an other-focused lover; they are self-focused lovers. The self-focused lover has sex for her own gratification. She only has sex when she wants to have sex. Feminism did much to make today's women in their thirties and forties self-focused lovers. They learned how to get themselves off and what they needed a partner to do to get them off.

A self-focused lover can separate sex from love. She knows when she wants it and does what she needs to do to get it. She may be a woman who primarily lives in her head, who regards sex as a means to balance herself out. Sex offers just the amount of transcendence she can handle. After a couple of hours of letting go, she's ready to go back up into her head.

These two approaches to being a lover might best be regarded as archetypes rather than indelible states. Many women incorporate parts of each, depending on how they feel and who they're with. Before Cathy had a baby, Bill experienced her as an other-focused lover, because she seemed to enjoy sex so much that she never turned him down. Unlike the traditional other-focused lover, who ascends to her partner's advances, Cathy maintained that she wasn't going to have sex unless she was sin-cerely interested. Since she had never faked interest to keep her relation-ship alive, she became what Bill would regard as a self-focused lover.

In my twenties, I measured my lovemaking from the perspective of a self-focused lover. If I got off, I'd feel the encounter was successful; if I didn't, I'd feel used. I regarded having an orgasm as a reliable measure of "good" love-making. Since no one was paying me to have sex, I felt no obligation to fake orgasm. Soon, something troublesome to my neat political analysis of sex arose. Men in whom I had little emotional interest could easily get me off, but men I cared about triggered so many crossed circuits that I'd remain in a jittery state of wanting. My telltale body seemed to be playing games with me. To repair the confusion, I'd tell the emotionally uninteresting men to get lost.

In my mind, I couldn't (or at least shouldn't) have sex without love. If it managed to slip in, I had to quickly banish it. I wouldn't allow myself to consider that combining sex with love is simply a cultural construct and not a universal practice among all humans. The only paradigm I allowed myself was the challenge of good sex amidst a backdrop of intricately woven and (at least potentially) loving emotions.

As I got older and more emotionally involved with my lovers, surrender became more interesting. Being self-focused was empty relative to completely letting go. The more I let go, the more I felt, and the more I found deep pleasure in making my partner feel good. As I found value in being other-focused, I gradually incorporated both perspectives into my best lovemaking. The thought of having sex just for sex was as dull as the thought of servicing a partner to cause him to like me more.

I realized that I might need to receive a lot of pleasure before I felt inspired to give. Nonetheless, giving was a delectable part of the experience, and if I didn't feel moved to give, something was missing. For lovemaking to be all I knew it to be, I had to both surrender and be surrendered to.

LIVING WITH A LOVER

If single people who live with their lovers were counted by the Census Bureau as "married" rather than "single," the numbers of single people would be significantly lower. Getting married is usually a conscious act, but living with one's lover may begin very unconsciously. Soon after he began dating Lucy, Greg would leave progressively larger quantities of his belongings at her place. What began as a toothbrush, some changes of underwear, and a couple of books gradually grew to fill half the drawers of her dresser, a walk-in closet, and a wall-sized bookcase. Eventually, Lucy decided that since Greg was spending every night with her, he might as well move in the rest of his things and pay a share of the rent.

Christie was completely unconscious that she'd be living with a lover when she moved into Ken's apartment. Writing a check for the first and last month's rent, as well as a security deposit, she took up residence as Ken's platonic roommate. After several weeks of talk over morning coffee, occasional shared meals, and sitting on opposite ends of the couch as they watched late-night TV, they began to acknowledge their mutual attraction. As they drifted to the center of the couch, they risked an all-or-nothing connection. If it didn't work out, the tension would be so thick one of them would have to move out. Their gamble worked, and eventually they married.

When I was twenty, my college boyfriend and I decided to live together. Our decision had nothing to do with marriage or a premarital trial. We simply liked each other, would rather sleep together than apart, and had a lead on a wonderful house in the Berkeley Hills. My parents went into major generation-gap shock, but eventually they came around to accept him and our decision. Nonetheless, our living together was simply that; it wasn't a precursor to anything more intense, committed, or romantic.

For many women, especially as they get older, deciding to live with a lover becomes fraught with symbolism and anxiety. They worry if they "give it away for free" whether they'll ever be paid back in wedding rings and happy-ever-after vows. In contrast, many women don't want to be married just yet or perhaps ever again, but do want the social intimacy of living with a lover. When you live with a lover, each day you wake up and decide to stay with each other, you reaffirm your relationship. There are no contracts; you stay because you want to.

Ultimately, living together challenges the value and purpose of marriage. When a woman chooses to live with her lover, but rejects marriage, she's saying she has no interest in having the state or organized religion meddle in her personal affairs. She's not concerned about legally sanctioned security; she'd rather call her own shots and pay her own way.

WOMEN WHO DON'T HAVE SEX

Negotiating sex, let alone relationships, isn't easy or even interesting for many of the women I spoke with. When I told Laura, the spunky fifty-two-year-old director of a non-profit environmental organization, that I was doing research on the sex lives of single women, she readily volunteered that she "doesn't do men." She quickly explained that she "doesn't do women either" and that she simply finds the social world of her work much more interesting than the bother of building a romance.

Equally dynamic Greta, a university professor in her early fifties, confides that she hasn't had sex in close to eight years. Does she miss it? "Not really." Some years ago she grew tired of being "manipulated, controlled and smothered" by men who were in search of "caretaker-mothers they could have sex with" and then build their own "little cocoon of dysfunctionality." Now, Greta assesses that the men of her status and stature are "dumpy or married or both" while the males she does find attractive (her students and hunky guys at the gym) are not appropriate. Besides, she says, "Who would want to risk catching one of those deadly diseases?"

Apart from self-contained, career-focused women like Laura and Greta, I also heard story upon story of single women who live lonely, often sexless, lives. Eliza, forty-two, reflects:

> There's something inside of me that's crying for intimacy . . . that's crying for peace . . . for an indelible spiritual, sexual, emotional connection. Instead I find myself setting limits, making sure I stay in my own bed, that my tongue stays in my own mouth—that I share feelings with safe friends. It's no fun being so tight. No woman should have to be this tight so much of the time. I just want to cry and shout and moan and scream and feel and respond and be responded to.

Finally, some women (and men) have been damaged by sex. Apart from rape, unwanted pregnancy, and sexually transmitted diseases, there are also subtler, more insidious injuries. Some women's bodies react with yeast infections, bladder infections and herpes outbreaks each time they have sex. They may claim they enjoy sex, but their bodies' negative response buys them "recovery time" until their next fateful episode. Jillian, a bright and personable actress who easily attracts men, twitched uncomfortably as she revealed that nearly every time she agrees to have sex, she gets so sore she's unable to have sex again for weeks:

> Having it hurt when I'm being penetrated is horrible, not just because it hurts, but also because I said "yes," while in that actual moment I am actually feeling "no." It's horribly frustrating to be finding something you thought you wanted be so painful you really don't want it after all.

Jillian then described the anxiety she feels in revealing to her partner that she no longer wants the very act she claimed to be interested in. To avoid being so "emotionally messy," she fakes interest.

I fake it until it feels like "yes." I don't let him know that his loving act was hurting me. I find that if I rub my clit real hard and focus on getting turned on, I can block out the pain.

Jillian dissociates by getting herself turned on. She so displaces the pain with sexual excitement that she even orgasms after these initially painful episodes.

Los Angeles sex therapist Tom Glover contends that many of us, like Jillian, get sexually excited by dissociating our minds from our bodies by entering a trance-like state through alcohol, drugs, or seduction. He encourages his patients to concentrate on living in the present rather than buoying themselves into an unconscious orgasmic state. By staying conscious of their bodies and their partner's body, sex can become a vehicle for deeper communication and not an empty and painful escape. Women like Jillian may find that by remaining cooler, by not trying to get turned on, they'll actually do much better for themselves.

THE SEX LIVES OF BIO-TIME-CLOCK WOMEN

Bio-time-clock women who want to have sex as well as have a baby may look at the different men in their lives as commodities. They have men who are their friends and confidants, men who can be called on to delight them sexually, and then there are the men they hope to convert into bill-paying husbands, if not semi-responsible sperm donors. Meanwhile, the men they date are much more interested in romance. They want a slow build to a full relationship of sexual, emotional, and spiritual intimacy. In their frenzied rush to get pregnant before their clocks run out, these women have no time for this slow building. According to Jannie, the forty-two-year-old massage therapist whose bio-time-clock is anxiously ticking:

I don't have the time I used to have to fall in love. I still very much want to be in love. I want to have a spiritual connection and all that, but I guess more than anything I want to have a baby. At this point I just really want a baby. If a man can't handle it, then I'm not going to be able to handle him.

According to Avram, fifty-one, a gregarious and worldly artist and teacher, the single bio-time-clock women he meets are "a pain in the neck! They don't really want to laugh and get close and have a good time. They just want your sperm and your bank account." Equally plagued by these women's single-minded thinking, Lawrence, forty-four, a talented actor, thought he was on the road to getting the family life he wanted when he attempted to build a relationship with a woman who was openly trying to get pregnant. He figured that if he grew to like her enough, it might ultimately be what he wanted. One menstrual cycle into it, he sensed he was simply being used as a sperm-donating object:

When I told her it wasn't working for me, she said it was fine—that we didn't have to keep seeing each other—but then begged me to keep having sex with her so that she could still keep trying for her baby! I felt so disregarded. . . .

Gina, thirty-seven, never for a moment had trouble attracting men. She recently drew up a list of each of her primary relationships, in which she and her partner were openly and actively seeing each other. Then she checked off those men who had become lovers. A peculiar pattern emerged. All through her twenties and early thirties, every "primary" easily became her lover. Since her early thirties most of her primaries had not become lovers. What was happening? Her boyfriends had begun to see her as a marriage time bomb.

Sexual connection with a primary implied a level of commitment that was so deep, it was like playing with fire. She and they knew that if a pregnancy resulted she would want to keep the baby. She told a gorgeous songwriter she'd recently met that they could use double condoms and a diaphragm and he still backed off. In his mind, she was too much trouble. He had already had one woman disappear with what might have been his baby, and he was terrified it could happen again.

So, like Gina, a lot of bio-time-clock women have sex with partners with whom it's clear that a primary relationship is out of the question. Then, it's safe to just be sexual. Their lovers are former boyfriends, men in their early twenties who enjoy no-strings-attached flings, men they meet on vacations, men who are married or otherwise committed.

Gina's single male counterparts in their mid-thirties through forties probably aren't having as much sex as they did fifteen to twenty years ago either. Back then, according to Ted, an attractive transportation planner in his mid-forties, "If a woman liked you, she'd go to bed with you on the first date. If she didn't, you didn't call her again because the message was that she wasn't interested." Now, Ted claims, women only have sex with men they consider "marriage material." That is, unless they judge the man to be totally out of the running—already married, too young, too old or from a different class or culture. Then they might just close their eyes and let themselves go.

SAFE SEX AND CONDOM-COMMITMENT GAMES

Straight talk about safe sex isn't easy at any time. And talking about safe sex and one's HIV status shouldn't be construed as an agreement to have sex. However, safe sex discussions, if they happen at all, are most likely to occur once the decision to be sexual is made. And once lovemaking begins, anxiety over breaking the mood can lead to unsafe activities.

Condom use, even in the age of AIDS, can be seen as a painful breech of trust among single heterosexuals. When a man and woman agree to become lovers, a partner's request to use condoms may suggest that the user is diseased or that the user suspects that his new lover could be diseased.

Using condoms can also presume a level of distrust. When Lisa and Gary met, they presumed each other was "safe" since they'd both come out of long, monogamous relationships. Lisa stayed on the pill, and to her, it seemed everything was under control. Not using condoms to Lisa presumed a level of trust that legitimized their relationship. Then, one evening Gary put on a condom and Lisa grew very suspicious. Was he seeing someone else? Had he violated their exclusivity?

For men and women like Lisa and Gary, exclusivity is supposed to insure not only emotional commitment but medical safety. Just the fear of having one's safe AIDS status violated can trigger intense emotional turmoil. Condoms have become widely accepted as an absolute requirement for safe gay sex (witness the dramatic lowering of new HIV infections among gay men), but they remain problematic among single heterosexuals. One reason may be that gay men more easily accept promiscuity in themselves and in their partners. They accept physical attraction as reason enough to want to have sex . . . and they accept that condoms are necessary for everyone to prevent the spread of infections.

Heterosexuals tend to think their own choices and behaviors are impervious to AIDS infections because sex between women and men often implies a certain exclusivity. If the sex is for procreation, the man wants to know that he is the only possible father and the woman wants to assure him of that so she can count on his financial support. If it's not yet for procreation, but might be someday, their sexual exclusivity becomes a measure of their commitment to being parents in the future.

WOMEN WHO MAKE LOVE WITH WOMEN

Many of us are not fully heterosexual nor fully homosexual. In a culture that condemns homosexuality, only those who are intensely homosexual become practicing lesbians. Certain traumas, however, can cause a woman who might otherwise be somewhere in the middle to assume a gay lifestyle. When Claudia's fiancé failed to show up at the sumptuous wedding her parents threw for her, she became so angry that she never again pursued intimacy with a man:

> I was so shell-shocked by being literally left at the altar, I could never again open my heart to a man. I came to regard all men as emotionally deficient. They were not to be believed and certainly not to be trusted. I don't think a woman would do this to another woman. I only trust women.

Maria's parents attempted to teach her the values of their homeland (Peru) while raising her in Los Angeles, but the boys she dated didn't respect her the way Peruvian men respect Peruvian women. Maria would be persuaded into sex before she was interested and would hate it so much that she'd break off the relationship. She stayed involved with her last boyfriend for a full eight months because he was as uninterested in sex as she was. Then one evening, she went to a restaurant with some friends and met a woman:

> I don't know how this happened, because I was never interested in women in that way. I had never before even met a lesbian. But this woman, she happened to be the owner of the restaurant, must have noticed me. She got my number from my friends and started calling me. I must have put her off for six weeks until finally I agreed to have dinner with her. She was so easy to talk to. I felt so comfortable with her. It was the first time in my life I really felt turned on. She asked me if I minded her seducing me. I sort of shook my head "no." She was incredible. I'd never felt so engaged in my life.

Identifying as lesbian has enabled Maria to feel more powerful. She openly enjoys sex and has effectively sidestepped the troublesome dynamics of heterosexuality. While she and Claudia may not be exclusively homosexual, a lesbian relationship fully meets their needs for engagement, intimacy, sex, and love.

Gay Men And Straight Women

Straight women may befriend gay men for companionship that is free of troublesome ulterior motives. The women may enjoy that he has more access to his feminine side and easily talks about food, fashions, emotions, and other men. Straight women may confide much more candidly in a gay man, sensing he won't take advantage of them sexually. They can have security and protection without the potential burden of his sexuality.

Some women, known pejoratively as fag hags, so enjoy the culture and language of gay men that their social worlds revolve largely around them. Eventually, a closeness may grow that wants to be addressed sexually. The woman then faces the challenge of making herself so compelling that he (at least in part) gives up his proclivities and his lifestyle to engage her. When a gay man commits to a straight woman, he keeps in the back of his mind the thought that there's always a safe haven of men he could be lovers with if she doesn't work out. Jamie faced this struggle with Dan, her gay lover.

He said he really wanted a family life and I wanted that, too, and I really loved him and so we got involved. He never really trusted me—he was always a little worried that if he got too close, he might lose control, that I might swallow him alive or something. And then his attentions were always somewhat divided since all the rest of his friends were gay men. He never gave that up.

Eventually, Jamie gave Dan up. For however safe she initially felt being friends, he was unable to commit to her in the ways she wanted from a life partner. While she still enjoys befriending gay men, she now holds them at more of a distance.

Insatiable Women: Women Who Like Sex An Awful Lot

Unlike Claudia, Maria, and Jamie, some women live at the opposite end of women's sexual repression. These women love the charge and challenge of being sexual with red-blooded, heterosexual men. Because our culture routinely represses women's sexuality, at the rare moments when a woman passes through the door to sexual fulfillment, her interest in more seems endless: that sex in the afternoon won't be enough—

that sex all weekend won't be enough–that it all just won't be enough!

Jana, twenty-six, loves sex. She meets men everywhere—in laundromats, supermarkets, bars, malls, parks. . . . And if she senses a certain spark from a man before the end of the day, they will become lovers. For her, having sex is an exchange of energy; it's a way to get close, and it doesn't particularly matter if she ever sees the guy again. She may seem like a Teflon lover, but she's just doing what she likes. She's open to a steady relationship, but Jana is sexually alive all day long:

> *A day doesn't feel complete unless I get turned on, am a turn-on for someone else, and get off. While I love being wanted, the last thing I want to feel is possessed, controlled, or trapped!*

Men's pornography celebrates the sexually liberated woman who wants it in all orifices at once. She's uninhibited, can't get enough, and she never gets hurt. Unlike Jana, she's oblivious to entrapment. Her ego is so vacant that she's a mechanical fantasy.

Because our culture is so sexually repressive to women, a woman like Jana, who is ecstatically interested in sex all on her own, is a bit of an anomaly. What's more likely for women are limited periods of frenzied sexual exploration. Marge, thirty-three, upon leaving a sexually vacant seven-year marriage, got herself invited to S/M and swing parties, and moonlighted as a phone-sex actress. She reports:

> *I want to plow through everything that has ever held me back sexually. I want to giggle, play, try new fun stuff, and just do it and do it and do it. . . . At this point, powerful sexual connections are so intense for me that it takes me days to pick up the pieces. Is that why women stay sexually repressed relative to men?*

Tammy, a high-powered Wall Street commodities trader, indulged in a series of workshops on tantric sex, extended sexual orgasm, and intimacy. She then abandoned her career to become what she gleefully calls a "trained slut." The intensity she once directed to making money now turns to the more compelling pursuit of hour-long full-body orgasms.

Women in our culture like Marge and Tammy get defeated by sex. They desperately want it, enjoy it, and yet afterwards, they don't do well picking up the pieces. When they surrender to their primal sexual natures, there's nothing left. Unlike men, for whom surrender converts into inspiration to be great, productive and bring home lots of bacon, women may crumble professionally.

THE SEX-LOVE-ATTENTION ROLLER COASTER

You might call them sex and love addicts, or women (and men) who like the chase more than the prize, or simply people who aren't particularly interested in settling down. Often they say that they're looking for someone special, that this time they're really ready to be serious and settle down, and yet they never settle for very long.

There are lots of people on sex-love-attention roller coasters, the result of a culture that touts new hot sex as a very desirable commodity. If you listen to the top forty love songs and watch the love-themed box office hits, you get the message that falling in love is really interesting, while being in a committed relationship gets old. Sex in a relationship may lose its charge after the first six months to a year, and so the roller coaster ride begins.

We may have been programmed for variety deep in our primate heritage. In a typical chimpanzee troop, the males stay interested in sex because different females go into estrus (heat) every couple of weeks. Under experimental conditions, all the females in a troop were given hormones so that they would display estrus characteristics all the time. While initially the males were interested and there was lots of sex, eventually sexual activity tapered off. The only thing the experimenters could do to increase sexual activity was to introduce a new set of hormonally stimulated females. Human females are sexually receptive year round, so they may be equivalent to the experiment's hormonally stimulated chimps. While our monogamous culture tells us to marry and mate for life, chimpanzees, the one primate whose DNA is ninety-nine percent the same as humans, lives in a thoroughly non-monogamous social system.

People who ride the sex-love-intimacy roller coaster are often regarded as unstable and immature, but perhaps all they're doing is listening to their primal craving for variety. The roller coaster riders might say they want to stop the ride, but their ups and downs have become so compelling that a long-term relationship pales in comparison.

Jay, forty-five, rides the E-ticket relationship roller coaster. He's forever meeting women who are all he's ever wanted: smart, sexy, talented, thin, with long, dark, curly hair. When he's met a new woman, all he can talk about is her. In the beginning, he's on the phone with her for two to three hours every evening, and the weekends are filled with non-stop lovemaking. Three weeks into his "this-is-finally-it" love affair, the fighting starts. She's trying to control him, he doesn't trust her, she doesn't really have a career, she's too self-absorbed and isn't emotionally available, and of course she says he isn't emotionally available. Soon it's hopeless, she really wasn't the right one and by the way, he wants to know, are there any parties this weekend where he might meet an available single woman?

The more I hear Jay's ever-absorbing dramas, the more I become convinced that for some people the ups and downs of the this-could-be-the-relationship-I've-always-wanted roller coaster are much more interesting than actually finding "the relationship." And then, who's to say that the goal of settling down is a better goal than the goal of dating around?

While sex in marriage does have the potential for being intense and deeply spiritual and emotional, the typical American couple makes love thirty to forty hours a year: a measly forty minutes a week. Many American marriages lack passion because they are products of lots of rules—rules for dating, rules for intimacy, rules for when it's right to do certain things, and rules for who works and who cares for children. Adhering to these rules may bludgeon spontaneity and an appetite for pleasure, keeping people from the truth of who they are and what would really please them.

Women Who Play As Men

Yolanda, fifty-three, says getting married in her late teens and being the caretaker for her husband and children totally burned out any interest she might have had in being a traditional wife again. Divorced for the last twenty-five years, she frequents bars and clubs that Mexican nationals in their teens and twenties go to for a good time. And Yolanda shows them a good time. She dances and flirts and raves about how these hunky guys find her so attractive. Sometimes she rents a room at a nearby hotel and invites one of them up for post-dance recreation. She's confident. She knows just what she wants and she knows just how to get it. She supplies the condoms, and they supply a passionate heat she never had when she was married.

Celeste, confident, successful and forty-three, delights in describing the men in her life as "boy toys." They are the ones who get attached, fall in love and whine for more attention. Meanwhile, she keeps them at bay, too absorbed in her high-powered career to empathize with their fluttering hearts.

A woman like Yolanda or Celeste can play with "boy toys" when all of her security needs are met. When she owns her own home, earns a good salary, and is a confident whole person in her own right, boys can be toys. These women can then defy all of the social norms, because they're not trying to impress anyone. They can play, let go, be wild and get down with guys from different social classes, cultures, and ethnicities. They can do the kinds of things they might never have dreamed of doing with a husband, like being tied up or exploring sadomasochistic fantasies.

Yolanda may eventually want more than flirtation and a safe-sex one-night stand, but for now she's angry at what her husband did to her and at the traditional cultural rules that tell women to play coy and tell men to control women. She's getting even with men. Though Yolanda chuckles over how the young men call and tell her they're in love, she admits there's little relationship potential there.

And in a quieter, more reflective moment, Celeste does confess she sometimes yearns for a more multidimensional relationship between equals. She'd like a lover she can respect, but meanwhile she's getting off by getting even.

OLDER WOMEN AND YOUNGER MEN

A growing number of older women prefer to build (and have built) serious relationships with younger men. These men appreciate them for being experienced, confident and sexually open. Traditionally, women trade "beauty power" for men's financial power. When the two opposite ends of the spectrum meet, and men who have yet to accumulate wealth or power connect with women who are past what our culture regards as their physical prime, something interesting happens. Communication is more direct and the exchange can be more honest.

Since it's a "lower-stakes trade," women are less likely to hold back. If the two are attracted to each other, there is really no reason to wait. The young men report that the women are confident lovers who know their own bodies and know how to satisfy men. And the women rave about the pleasures of being with a hard-bodied young stud who is anything but set in his ways.

Shayla, gorgeous, brilliant, and thirty-six, knows that her twenty-year-old lover is not marriage material, but nonetheless admits that he's been much easier to get close to than men her age. Because she hasn't run him through all of her "is-he-appropriate filters," she just enjoys him:

He's wonderful—his body is wonderful—he's brainy and he's sensitive. I'm just enjoying him. I don't like being alone. I don't like sleeping alone. I'd rather spend time with him than lie in bed lonely until I meet someone appropriate. . . .

Does Shayla have a timetable for meeting someone appropriate? Of course not. She regards her twenty-year-old as a transitional lover who, though inappropriate, certainly meets her needs for companionship, emotional sharing and sex. Her behavior is, in fact, quite logical for a human being. Despite the fact that her culture tells her he's not appropriate, would it be better for her to stay at home with her vibrator and keep getting dumped by potential Mr. Rights who judge her wrong?

Gloria, voluptuous and forty-eight, finds her twenty-eight-year-old lover, Mark, to be a wonderful respite from the thirty years she spent with her high-powered financial-genius husband. Mark is a low-keyed yoga teacher who can barely scrape together $300 to rent his small ashram room. Gloria raves about how peaceful she feels with Mark, and then quietly mutters that there's something really sexy about a high-powered financial genius and that she's still looking. While being with a much younger man may sound dreamy on paper, the emotional realities of being with a man who doesn't exude power and confidence can be unsatisfying.

WOMEN WHOSE LOVERS ARE MUCH OLDER MEN

Women may be drawn to much older men by their power, their wisdom, sometimes their money, and always their devout attention. When a woman is being romanced by the head of Dynamegalomaxitron, Inc. and he takes her calls on his private line in the middle of a top-level management meeting, she feels special. For however young, impoverished, and powerless she is, she holds a certain power over him and she relishes it. Meanwhile, men of her age and status are too busy trying to get ahead to be able to take time out from work to romance her.

Older men may benefit by feeling they can defy gravity, or at least their age, and access immortality. If they can capture the interest and attention of someone much younger, they feel they've reclaimed youthfulness. Her body has not yet succumbed to gravity, yet she admires him without judgment, and she often has less emotional baggage than women his age. With her, he may feel he can put his own bags down.

Marlene was enrolled in a senior seminar led by Dennis, a sensitive, worldly, and inspiring university professor. She'd stay after class and meet with him in his office to discuss her research project. She loved their conversations:

He listened so well—he was always so interested in what I uncovered. . . . Whenever we talked, he made me feel that I made so much sense. None of the guys I dated treated me that way. They were too saddled with their own projects to ever listen to mine. All they wanted from me was my body. They always put so much pressure on me, while with Dennis I could relax . . .

Marlene was literally in shock when, a week after graduation, Dennis made an unsuccessful pass at her:

I turned pale, and became sweaty and tongue-tied, when he reached over to kiss me. I could not believe that this safe, engaging, ever-adoring man had been thinking carnal thoughts about me! My whole world had turned upside down!

What Marlene had considered a safe haven was suddenly eclipsed by the turbulent world of men, women, and sex. But after several post-college escapades that lacked the candor and connection she had experienced with Dennis, she contacted him. She so enjoyed the dynamics of their relationship that for many years she continued finding much older men (who she would never consider marrying) very appealing.

These relationships' dynamics may include mentoring her, and/or filling her needs for a thoroughly loving and supportive father. The couple's difference in age and status means there is no competition. They appreciate each other for what they don't have in themselves. He likes being adored, and she's naturally adoring to someone who seems so brilliant and worldly.

His ideas about sex may be more complex and elaborate than hers. She may be offended by what he's interested in. Marlene recalls:

Sex with Dennis was very weird. He'd grunt and growl and make very weird sounds. I think it was supposed to be some kind of exchange of animal energies. He was rough and wanted me to do strange things. While I loved him dearly, our appetites were so different that we never really could connect sexually.

Marlene never considered marrying Dennis, she says:

No, we were honestly in very different places in our lives. While I may have made him feel young and he may have made me feel brilliant, not all of me needed or for that matter wanted all of him. Being with him filled a certain appetite, but I never, ever put him in the category of men I would marry.

LIFE AS A MISTRESS: BEING A MARRIED MAN'S "OTHER WOMAN"

Several women I spoke to have been lovers of married men. Many claim they wouldn't do it again, while some extol the virtues of being "the other woman." Generally these relationships are clandestine. A single woman isn't likely to tell her parents, friends or co-workers that she's met the most fabulous married man and that she's never had better sex, communication, or a deeper sharing of emotions. If she did, she'd probably be criticized for having low self-esteem and being stupid.

These relationships, then, remain private. Thus the couple can stay in a netherworld of deep romance, unhindered by practicalities or plans for a public future that would include things like weddings, marriage, and babies.

Feminism, interestingly, factors strongly in the creation of relationships between married men and single women. While the men may appreciate their feminist wives' strength and sense of self, they may also enjoy being the one to make and break all the dates with their mistresses. Typically busier and with more family responsibilities, the men may call all the shots. The mistresses may also be feminists. Feminism may have caused them to so value their freedom that they have little interest in being a full-time housekeeper/care-taker kind of wife. They'd rather the time spent with their lover be for deep sharing and passionate sex.

Women who become mistresses often report being initially oblivious to the possibility of a sexual connection between themselves and their married lover, whom they regarded as "safe." The women comfortably enter into friendships, confide secrets, and build trust. They find themselves much more relaxed around these men, who seem to have none of the ulterior, "get her into the sack" motives of horny single men. Julianne, thirty-eight, described how she got involved with Bart, her married lover:

Initially, I wasn't sure he was sexually interested in me. The first time he hugged me, he placed his lips against mine and breathed gently. We didn't actually kiss. I felt different than I'd ever felt before—fresh, new and genuine. We were navigating a whole new territory of relationship: something deeply emotional, spiritual, intellectual—and perhaps slightly sensual.

When we'd get together it was like we already knew each other. Our heads would playfully knock each other, our legs would tangle and our spirits would sing. A bond was building between us. I wasn't too conscious of what was happening nor what it would ultimately mean. It happened without calculation or discussion. It was like a force larger than us stepped in and melded our hungry spirits.

The first time he lifted off my blouse and undid my bra, I surged with a shy innocence. Was this okay? He assured me it was, and I believed him. I felt like a teenager exploring womanhood for the first time. We were both virgins exploring this new world together. All directions were possible and no road maps existed.

Some single women find that being able to experience intimacy without the confines of an encompassing and possessive relationship can be a useful transitional phase. They can gain confidence as lovers and in their ability to feel deeply. By using an unavailable (e.g. married) man as a stepping stone, they can eventually develop an appetite for a man that could become all theirs.

Some women contend that they prefer being mistresses. To them, the life of a second woman is much more interesting than being any one man's wife. Mistresses have a status all of their own. When the "master" visits the mistress, he does so because he really enjoys her company. She makes him feel special, and he relishes it.

Mistresses are freer than wives. They are not expected to take on so much of a man's identity, and they don't feel so squelched by his power. Every time they see their lover, it's an exciting treat. They don't have to live with him. They can just savor him.

POLYGAMY/MAN SHARING

Some women, rather than being a clandestine mistress, openly share a man with another woman. While a measly 50,000 women in the United States are in polygamous marriages (they are largely unaffiliated Mormons), seventy-five percent of the world's cultures offer the option of polygamy. Seventy-three percent are polygynous (one male and at least two females) while just two percent are polyandrous (one female and more than one male).

Polygamy, like monogamy, does not come easily. When a new wife is added, there is often friction. The first wife may feel inadequate, worrying that she isn't enough of a woman for her husband. Generally, it's a lot more fun to be the new wife. Being new, she's seen as interesting, desirable, and as the most loved.

It can take a tremendous amount of generosity and trust for a first wife to accept, let alone befriend, a new woman in her household. Interestingly, women who stay in polygynous marriages find that they can have the best of both being married and being single. They belong to a family, have a lover, and yet are not as tightly bound to social identification as their husband's wife. Moreover, they have a community of co-wife sisters to share secrets as well as housework and child care.

What might it be like to be the new woman? Rachel, who is often open to new adventures, described her experience of being courted by a couple (Wayne and Cheri) she met at a party:

As I got ready to leave I told Wayne and Cheri that I enjoyed being with them and hoped we could get together again. It seemed that they had already conferred over me and were in agreement. Since Wayne had found me attractive, he had me talk to Cheri. Cheri approved of me, which set off a green light for further contact. Their negotiation was so simple and so open! My ears were perked for what else would follow.

The following morning Wayne and Cheri called to invite me to go dancing. The evening was unlike any other. They both greeted me warmly and we left to go to one of their favorite clubs. We got a table and Wayne sat between Cheri and me. We ordered drinks, chatted for a while and then Cheri encouraged me to dance with Wayne. We danced formally for several brief minutes and then lapsed into delicious sensual hugging. Meanwhile, Cheri danced with other partners while positioning herself in such a way that she could see our every move.

Back at our table Wayne snuggled in close to me. His hands were in my hands and then they were all over my thighs and legs. I felt a little uncertain as deeper levels of excitement surged through me. I looked up and Cheri looked just as excited as I felt. Wayne hadn't ignored her for a second. We were all in the same intimate moment. I had never before had a woman offer me her husband and all three of us totally enjoyed the experience.

Wayne and Cheri have created a marriage that gives them both freedom and security; with each other's permission, they are free to take on additional lovers. Rachel was seen as good for Wayne, good for Cheri, and good for Cheri and Wayne's relationship. The lust that Wayne and Rachel shared was far from dangerous; rather, it was exciting. Wayne and Cheri would stay married, while Rachel's involvement with them could simply add juice to their lives.

Jealousy is the emotional glue that shows us that we matter to each other. And it can wreak havoc in multiple partner relationships. An ancient, primal impulse, jealousy can be triggered by anger, fear, loss of self-esteem or physical/emotional separation. Sex educator Dr. Harvey Lampel contends that "the root cause of jealousy is exclusion. Having multiple partners doesn't in and of itself create jealousy. It's only when one partner is ignored in favor of someone else." A woman can give her husband permission to date another woman and feel increased excitement in her marriage. If, however, the husband excludes his wife from his affairs, it's very likely that she will feel jealous.

According to San Francisco therapist Isadora Allman, "What makes open relationships work is the convergence over agreements." A couple like Wayne and Cheri could agree to tell all and feel comfortable seeing all. This agreement doesn't by design prevent jealousy; instead, it allows outside love interests to add to the primary couples' excitement. Perhaps in the course of lovemaking, Wayne might tell Cheri how turned on he felt when he was dancing with Rachel. Wayne's excitement might make Cheri want him even more. But their relationship might break down if Cheri found a man she liked much better than Wayne and kept him a secret. If Wayne found out, he would know his marriage was in trouble because Cheri hadn't told him everything.

SEX WITH FRIENDS

Many women who claim to be seeing nobody special or no one at all do nonetheless have sex. They have sex with former lovers, and in no-strings-attached agreements with friends who have never been real lovers. Just about every woman I spoke with who'd been single for a while had men in her life. Some of these women had much more intimacy going with friends than many committed couples share with each other.

During the lulls of her search for a Mr. Pretty Good, Giselle, an intense twenty-eight-year-old designer, gets together with the sexy soap opera star she met four years ago at her Hollywood health club. A solitary Jacuzzi jet massage paled in comparison to what this man could do with his two hands for her sore muscles. Soon she managed to show up every evening just about the time he'd get off the set for more Jacuzzi-inspired manipulations. One day he reached under her swimsuit; she yanked his fingers out, warning him that he had gone a little too far. In her mind, there were boundaries for where casual friends could touch and what was reserved for a true lover. The next time her sexy soap star reached, she thought it over and let herself melt. The Jacuzzi bubbles would shield her from curious onlookers, and if it felt good, why not?

Carmella, a twenty-seven-year-old waitress, would be the first to admit that she hasn't yet gotten over Karl, the guy she lived with for two years and who is, in her mind, the best lover on the planet. Every month or so she drops by his house for dinner or a tennis game or both. Afterwards she nestles on his couch in such a way that it looks like she couldn't possibly have the energy to drive home. As the ritual proceeds, Karl notes she looks pretty sleepy. Perhaps she'd like to stay over. She agrees that she's really sleepy and then saunters into the bathroom, finds her old toothbrush, and gets ready for bed. They lie in bed stone-faced for about thirty seconds, until her body somehow slithers over his. While he says they shouldn't be doing this anymore—that this keeps them from finding true-blue marriage material—they keep doing it and it keeps feeling good.

Bonnie, unlike Carmella and Giselle, contends that being sexual without deep-felt emotions and a growing relationship "feels cheap." For a couple of years, she had weekly lunches that spilled over into much of the afternoon with Scott, a married banker. "Scott's main attributes," according to Bonnie, "are that he is reasonably bright, usually interesting, and a communicative and skilled lover." While Scott was willing to see Bonnie forever, after a while Bonnie lost interest. While the sex itself never stopped being wonderful and the conversations remained reasonably interesting, Bonnie wanted more. She wanted to be lovers with a man she really loved—and for that, she decided, she would be willing to wait.

VACATION SEX

Rather than connecting with unavailable men in town, some women manage to have the sum total of their lovemaking occur when they're out of town and/or on vacation. Like clockwork, every time Dana went scuba diving in the Caribbean, she'd meet the most wonderful man. Several times a year she would come back with gorgeous pictures of deep-sea corals, pufferfish, and some very hunky guy. In town, she was busy working as an accountant at a prestigious law firm and had no time for anybody. All she did was work, work out, work around the house, and go shopping. When she'd arrive in the Cayman Islands, her social filtering system completely altered. Suddenly, she was interested in diving partners, after-diving dinner companions, and after-dinner snuggling companions. And she easily found them. For some reason, they never came home with her. The best she and they ever did was arrange to meet at some other gorgeous island the same time the following year.

Women with the biggest appetites for vacation sex are those like Dana, whose home lives are otherwise committed. They have no reason to disrupt anything at home to accommodate someone they found wonderful on vacation. They know how to savor certain moments without fantasizing about more. They have rubber band boundaries; they can be very open for the weekend, but then snap back to size when they return home.

Yvette, unlike Dana, thought she'd found the love of her life when she met Paulo on a rickety second-class bus in Patzcuaro, Mexico. They shared dinner that evening and snuggled together in his hotel room afterwards. He was on his way back to the U.S. while she was headed deeper into Mexico. It didn't matter, he was perfect; this connection wouldn't fade. Several months later he met her in Oaxaca and again, he was all that she could ever imagine wanting in a man. Later, she moved to Boston and would visit him in New York. As always the chemistry, the connection, and the conversations were exquisite. After several years of rendezvous with Paulo which never led to more, she forced herself to surmise:

> I never really had a relationship with Paulo. Over the last many years, we never spent more than a couple of days together. I really don't know what he does with dirty laundry, or what he's like when he's working a forty-hour week. I only know what he's like on vacation. I only know him as perfect.

Women like Yvette experience such silver-lined sensations with the men they meet on vacations that any male they might happen to encounter in their day-to-day lives seems dull. Their appetite for savoring at a distance safely keeps them from sampling a dirty-laundry-filled, potentially possessive relationship that might lead to marriage.

SEX AT WORK

The other side of sexual harassment in the workplace is consensual sex with co-workers. Plenty of people receive sexual advances at work and then beg for more. As opposed to sexual harassment, the components for sex on the job are discretion, mutual consent and mutual respect for boundaries. Sex on the job happens in closets, bathrooms, after hours, on location, and in the field. Many people meet their spouses on the job, while plenty of women who don't happen to be married have been known to have sex on the time clock.

Natalie was Bill's right hand during the eight years they worked together. She was young, black, and gorgeous. He was white, middle-aged, and traditional, but with a wild side. Between them there was a thick, amazing chemistry. He was the CEO and she was his secretary. During the day, they got things done, and when everyone left, they satisfied each other. They were a team, and everyone respected their track record. Because Bill needed Natalie, he protected her, trusted her, and gave her special concessions. She was able to take month-long vacations, work flexible hours, and wear whatever she pleased.

When Jennie, a surgical nurse in her forties, works the night shift, there's often some down time when she and one of the interns squeeze into a closet and get each other off. It makes the long shifts go faster, and as far as she is concerned:

> *If you can get away with it, why not? If it wasn't for these guys, I'd never get it from anybody. At this point in my life, I'm not looking for a relationship. The quickies I get on the job do me just fine.*

While members of The Lifestyles Organization (a national swingers group), expect to have sex at their conventions, their convention behavior is certainly not the exception. Barbara, an attractive television executive, finds that at her professional conventions:

> *As soon as I slip out of my business suit and go down to the bar or out to the pool, I'm considered fair game. The men, single and married alike, presume*

that because I'm there, I'm interested and available. It's like a fantasy world for the weekend.

As long as strings stay unattached, professional women like Barbara can pretty much have whoever they'd like for the night, if not the whole convention weekend.

WOMEN WHO HAVE SEX WITH THEMSELVES

I don't know how many there are, but my guess is if you're a woman reading this book, you're probably one of them. Having sex with yourself is a way to feel good, relieve tension, and refocus. Through masturbation you can discover or reconfirm your body's rhythms, so the next time you're with a partner more of what you know is possible might happen. Then again, your body's rhythms with a partner may be humming to a whole different song than when you're on your own.

On your own, you can peak yourself fifty times before you go over the edge, you can slip over the first time, or just loll in mid-level turn-on. You can use a vibrator, add a dildo, play music, light candles, throw out the dildo, unplug the vibrator, blow out the candles and go au naturale with your own fingers!

What used to be many women's best-kept secret until *Sliver* came out was using a perfectly heated stream of water while lolling in a bathtub. While the movie only pictured Sharon Stone's steamy face, the rest of the shot might have revealed her crunched somewhat under the faucet with her clitoris in line to receive the full effects of the warm stream. Women with a small hardware budget can hook up ten-foot hoses off of their shower nozzles and control the flow by bending the hose!

Masturbation can advance to another level when it's combined with phone sex. And phone sex may be one of the last remaining truly safe ways to have sex with another person. Kendra met Alan at a boisterous party where they danced, chased each other from room to room and basically got themselves real steamy. As the party wound down, Kendra and Alan locked eyes. The heat between them was barely endurable as he shoved his phone number into her open hands and told her to call him as soon as she got home. She did and what followed, according to Kendra, was the first (but certainly not the last) time she had phone sex:

It was really amazing. I think I learned more about him as a lover than I ever would have in person with the lights off and with our voices hushed. He told me just what to do to him and since he was doing the actual doing and not me, I agreed to all kinds of things I probably wouldn't do with anyone, especially with someone I just met.

When he asked me what I wanted, it first seemed kind of dumb since I was really doing myself. For a while I considered faking it—after all, he'd never know. Then I decided that I might get more out of this if I was completely authentic. I was extremely direct, told him just what I liked and what I wanted to hear. I must say it was one of the more intense sexual experiences I'd ever had. . . .

Kendra discovered her own impish and confident sexual voice through phone sex with Alan. He never played a major role in her life, but being a telephone seductress has become her ongoing hobby. Anyone she's dating who seems open to such play gets a lot. When she's really bored, she calls men who advertise in her newspaper's voice mail personals column and plays wild woman, temptress, or coy but seductive little girl. She rarely meets these guys—it's just a fun, safe way to let off steam!'

BEING PART OF AN INTIMATE COMMUNITY

What can you do if you want intimacy, belonging, relationship, and love, and you're burned out and/or distrustful of ever meeting your life-long soul mate? You can build or become part of an intimate community. An intimate community can be as safe and simple as people who celebrate holidays together and do what they can to meet each other's needs for friendship, hugs, and support. Communities can also share deeply felt emotions and sexual intimacy.

I am part of an "electronic intimate community" that stays in touch through telephones, faxes, E-mail, and modems. We also see each other at classes, conferences, workshops, gatherings, and parties.

Is being in such a community enough? Liza, thirty-eight, a Venice Beach painter, put that question to the test. Her community life was dotted with intermittent casual sex, work, and friends, which sustained her until she met Dave, a thirty-nine-year-old photographer. Connecting with Dave awakened in her the promise of a deep emotional, spiritual, multidimensional relationship. What had seemed like an abundant and fulfilling community life suddenly seemed thin and cheap, relative to what life with him promised.

A couple of weeks into the relationship, Dave dropped Liza, leaving her writhing in confusion. She was turbulent, not so much over wanting or missing him as over this rekindled desire to be in the intense kind of relationship he'd promised. Perhaps her community had mitigated the need to have one man be her one and only. Given a whiff of that old romantic dream, she found there was something in her that still wanted it.

SEX AND NESTING

In this chapter we've seen one example after another of single women who find and/or create safe situations to meet their social, sexual, and emotional needs. Often they get involved with unavailable, though comforting and likable men. Women opt for such men because they are sexually repressed. If a woman expressed her sexuality the same way as a man, she wouldn't fear being possessed and controlled. He wouldn't treat her as a sex object and then disregard her afterwards. Pregnancy would be considered something she generated herself. He wouldn't be called upon for finances or protection; no one would know it was his seed inside of her.

Despite how feminism and the sexual revolution encouraged women to handle sex as casually as men handle sex, sex for women still triggers dependency. When emotional bonding occurs in a sexual relationship, women's primal desires to nest emerge. Even today, as more women build their own nests and have no need to trade sex for nesting materials, women like bullheaded, adventurous Marge reveal:

> I've got to admit that when I do spend a lot of time with a lover, lots of emotion in me gets released—I don't want to let go—I want him to really be there for me.

Alice, a thirty-seven-year-old physical therapist, recently faced her own fears of becoming involved with someone who could marry her when she got involved with an otherwise-committed man. She began to wonder if it would be enough to accept involvement with a man who will never father her children and can only see her in the afternoons:

Do I really truly not want to be supported by a man? Do I really truly want to have kids outside of a marriage? Do I really truly want to be financially independent forever? Is it okay that I never spend the night with my lover? I am not sure. . . .

Powerful, independent women like Alice find the most comfort with men that are not too available—until they step back and look at the blandness of the life they've carved out, or they get attached. Then their dependency needs kick in and they want the man they love to be available.

THE ZILLION-DOLLAR QUESTIONS

How, in this culture, can you be vulnerable, powerful, independent, and a fully integrated woman who is thoroughly sexy? How do you both express and protect your femininity and yet be an emergent woman? How do you satisfy your own legitimate sexual needs and be neither a powerhouse nor a pushover? In the next chapter we'll begin to answer these questions as we consider ways to make peace with yourself.

Chapter 9

Making Peace With Yourself

⌄•⌄

The Search For Solutions

When I began researching *Women Who May Never Marry* five years ago, I faced skepticism. I was warned that if I couldn't find appealing, viable solutions for this dreary, depressing, perhaps unsolvable "problem," no one would pay attention to my observations.

As an educator, I was initially focused on raising awareness. I wanted all the women who were anxious about not being married to realize that society had changed—and that we are all products of that change, as well as instruments for further change. I wanted them to stop blaming themselves for cultural changes that had minimized the social and economic needs for marriage while intensifying standards for good partner communication. I hoped they might stop trying to fit themselves with social-sexual straitjackets and start fully loving themselves just as they are. Finally, I wanted them to be free to see the men in their lives as worthy of their friendship and love, whether or not they became their husbands.

Already these concepts don't seem as revolutionary as they did when I began this project. Many more women, especially as they grow older, profess less interest in marriage. A Scripps Howard poll conducted in mid-July 1993 found that just fifty-one percent of single American women want to get married someday. (While ninety-three percent of women between eighteen and twenty-four want to marry, this desire fades down to seventy percent of women between twenty-five and thirty-four. Just fifty-three percent of women between thirty-five and forty-four are interested in marrying, and the appeal plummets to a sparse ten percent for retirement-age single women.) When I began researching this book, few women would agree to be interviewed once they heard my title. Among the few exceptions were the feisty black single mothers who were then my students at a community college in Watts. In their world, a woman takes full responsibility for going after whatever she wants. To them, the "retro-feminist strategies" that women perfected in West L.A. workshops were like a language from another planet. By the early '90s, women's attitudes had so changed that everywhere I went, women would freely offer me their stories and invite me to call them for more. The focus of the book shifted from "why single women are single" to "how women live now."

In the last eight chapters, we've examined the social, economic, and political changes that created the gap between how we were raised and how we now live. We went on to examine solutions from other times and places, including state-financed mothering for single Russian women after WWII, extended families for single Yucatec Mayan women, and the joys and freedoms of spinsterhood for 19th-century American women. We looked at the realities of being a bio-time-clock woman and evaluated the opportunity to make a family life without a provider/protector husband. We sorted through some of the multimillion-dollar singles industry's "how-to-get-married strategies," including changing your body, your behavior, your approach, and your techniques. Then we looked at the dilemmas men face in a changing world. We listened to thoughtful men who are aware that their disinterest in lucrative, full-time jobs may well cost them a traditional romantic relationship. Finally, we looked at the many ways single women avert the pain of being alone. We noted how some make themselves extraordinary, how others design their own magical worlds, and how many have fine-tuned ways to attain intimacy but remain free, by picking boy toy, long-distance, married, or part-time lovers who can't control them .

This chapter focuses on internal emotions. You are invited to look at yourself—to examine how you got here, to pay attention to dark patterns and emotions, and then embrace every bit of what you see. Instead of lying, making excuses, and living as if Mr. Right were just around the corner, you'll be invited to celebrate yourself just as you are.

Make Peace With Yourself: Live Fully Today

It's time to change your attitude. You are the person you wanted to be. Make peace with yourself—with the conscious and not-so-conscious decisions you have made that have caused you to be single today. In acknowledging these decisions, you can also acknowledge the world that has played no small part in shaping you. By making peace with yourself, you can be free to marry or not marry and feel equally good about yourself. It is better to honestly accept that you may never marry than to live forever tied to the "Princess Syndrome," believing that someday a prince will arrive to sweep you away.

Accept that being in a monogamous, heterosexual relationship is not necessarily a happy ending. Acknowledge the ways that intimacy already exists in your life—and appreciate your achievements. Love yourself today, embrace the community you have, and stop believing some guy will appear out of nowhere and flashdance you out of poverty and loneliness. You must live in the present and fully take charge of your life for the duration—not just until you get married.

Accept yourself as a woman who may never marry. For many women, marriage implies social acceptability and financial security. The fantasy of marriage to a man of means allows the poor working girl the promise of a secure life in a beautiful home. Even the woman with a viable career puts her emotional and sexual needs on hold, sensing she should wait until marriage to be "whole."

Stop putting your life on hold, and take steps to achieve the financial means to buy that car, condo, house, boat, station wagon, or summer home. Make a real home for yourself. Start right away by buying those satin sheets, monogrammed towels, china table settings and flatware. Take that nice vacation and throw yourself a big party.

Accept that you may never have children with that mirage of a husband. Have the baby you always wanted on your own. Or appreciate the other creations you have delivered from your feminine center. Expand your notions of what it means to create, and what it means to mother.

Give yourself the freedom to live fully every day, including eating all you want and having sex with whomever you'd like without leveraging it for a commitment. Let the men in your life—and yourself—be. You can then stop dressing to attract a Mr. Right and start dressing for yourself and for the people who actually are in your life. Celebrate all your long-standing friendships and connections with men and stop trying to make every "stranger across a crowded room" into all and everything. Stop imagining there's more to a relationship than there actually is, and begin to make peace with yourself.

Ultimately, this is about honesty. Give up encumbering fantasies and construct a life in which not marrying won't be seen (or experienced) as a loss. By facing who you are, where you've been, and admitting that you may never marry, you'll recapture your power. These steps are far beyond a quick-fix into a marriage trap; they are a prescription for life-long happiness.

You can achieve happiness whether or not you marry if you:

1. Let yourself be.
2. Let those around you be.
3. Stop hyping yourself up.
4. Stop escalating things.
5. Stop playing every man you meet for all or nothing.
   a. Let married men become real friends rather than dismissing them as not worth your time.
   b. Let men you are not attracted to be friends.
   c. Stop feeling that every man you associate with has to be husband material to be worth associating with you.
6. Open up your community of intimacy to women, to men with whom you would not want or could not have a romantic relationship. Let all of these people be your "family."

FACE UP TO ROMANTIC IMPERATIVE

Considering the emphasis our culture places on falling in love, it's no wonder many of us succumb to the This-Is-It Syndrome. Here, the romantic imperative takes hold as women rapidly read "relationship perfection" into someone they've just met. Some of the most professional, financially secure, and outwardly confident women have been known to fall apart when a This-Is-It man comes into their lives. Elisa, thirty-six, an otherwise self-sufficient stockbroker, sounded completely rattled when she told me about the new man in her life:

> I got so wired talking to Walter last night I couldn't sleep for hours. All my defenses start crashing. It's like I've finally met my soul mate. . . . It's so powerful when we're together and way too painful when we're apart.

This-Is-It feelings rarely last. Rather than really helping a woman like Elisa feel better about herself, This-Is-It feelings are more likely to lead to depression when she finds out this isn't it.

Some time ago, I ran a personals ad in a local paper and was profoundly struck by the extreme all-or-nothing attitude my callers and I practiced on each other. If there was a comfortable or exciting connection over the phone, my respondents would literally beg to meet as soon as possible. At the vast majority of these meetings, we'd immediately sense that this wasn't it and try to get out as soon as possible.

The tenor of these meetings seemed to reveal the conditions of romance in modern America. If "This Is It," we are prepared to drop everything, and if this isn't it, then there's no place for this new person in our lives. This attitude sets us up for an "addiction to love" that makes us think we should accept nothing but the real thing. It also sets us up for loneliness.

To test this attitude, I called up one of my respondents and reported I had already met someone I liked an awful lot (which was true) and was wondering if he'd like to get together just as friends. Over the phone he agreed, almost relieved that he wasn't going to be judged on an all-or-nothing basis. He then claimed to be too busy to meet for at least a couple of weeks. I knew full well that if I had presented myself as interested and available, he would have managed to meet in a matter of days.

Once you decide you no longer need to be saved or be transformed by the feelings of love, you can then feel peaceful whether or not you have a partner. It may take a complete ideological transformation to give up the notion that we need an "Other" to feel whole, capable, and complete. We need to consider that our neurotic need to "glom" onto someone may not be good for us or for our "glomees." In cultures where children are raised communally, such as on the Israeli kibbutz, parent-child ties tend to be less intense than in the American nuclear family. It would seem that a reduced focus on an "Other" in childhood would in turn reduce the need to make one's adult partner an all-encompassing "Other." My prediction is that we'd see less obsessive, less romantic, and less possessive relationships in a culture where there isn't as intense a need for the "Other" to fill all that one's parents did or did not provide.

The next step may be to look at our bio-physiological urges. Perhaps we might rethink the ways in which our genetically determined bio-chemical responses (the release of phenylethylamine [PEA], adrenaline, dopamine, serotonin) cause what we interpret to be intense love and passion. The simple presence of endorphins brings on feelings of attachment, tranquility and stability. Though Top Forty hit songs and Hollywood's illusion machine reinforce the myth of perfect love, our belief in it may in fact be keeping us from the peace we all deserve.

TELL YOUR STORY

In the course of researching this book, I found that when I offered women (and men) the opportunity to tell their whole stories as completely as they could, they began to accept themselves. Initially I asked such questions to gather stories to support theories I was developing, but eventually I offered private sessions and workshops for uncovering one's life story.

Telling your story can be very powerful. When a story elicitor focuses total attention on you, asking questions in an interested, but non-judgmental way, you may begin to recognize some patterns on your own. On the other hand, not examining your motives may result in blindly attempting to cram yourself into the latest sexy-self-sufficient-retro-feminist-flirt paradigm. Chances are you'll eventually feel miserable as a result.

I recommend that you tape record your story and arrange to have it transcribed as well. You can use a storytelling session to better see your relationship patterns and their origins. Sharing life stories can also be a wonderful way to build a relationship. When my partner, Don, and I first met, listening to and telling each other our stories was one of the most enjoyable and intimacy-building things we did.

To tell your sexuality/relationship story, have an undistracted partner ask you the following questions:

What were your first images of girls vs. boys? (What were the differences? How did you learn them?)

How did you feel about being male/female? How did you reckon that with your actual gender?

Were you affected by feminism and the sex role revolution? How? Did the changes make you feel more or less comfortable?

What kind of effect do sex roles have in your life today?

What were your early images of what sex would be like?

How did your first sexual experiences reckon with these images?

What have you learned about sex that you wish you knew then?

Decision Making In Your Family Of Origin:

Who had control?

Who was most powerful?

Who controlled finances? How?

What kind of relationship was there between power and work?

Who controlled the leisure time or social world?

Who controlled the emotional life? How?

What was the relationship between religion and power?

Who controlled the children and how?

What parts of each of your parents have you absorbed?

In what areas was power divided?

Now, Answer These Questions For Your Current Or Most Recent Life-Partner Relationship:

How do the dynamics in your parents' relationship compare to the dynamics in the relationships you've created?

Tell Your Relationship History:

For each significant relationship, answer:

How did you meet?

What drew you together?

What did you like about each other? What was difficult?

How were you similar? How different?

How did you deal with differences?
What were the best parts?

What caused it to end? Would that cause still be a reason for ending a relationship?

What did you learn?

REWRITE YOUR STORY

Once you tell your relationship/sexuality story, the next step is to rewrite it. To rewrite your story, you need to decide who you now want to be. You can be a woman who is in a committed relationship with one man she may someday marry, a woman who primarily delights in being on her own, a woman who is in love with another woman, or a woman who has multiple partners. . . . Now that you know the ending, just tell the parts of your story that telescope to the conclusion you want. Write this story down. Read it to yourself. Make it your story. Make it your life.

FACE UP TO FEELING INCOMPLETE

Perhaps you understand that marriage isn't necessary for your social, emotional, or economic survival. If you still feel a nagging incompleteness, answer the following series of exercises, which may help you isolate and ultimately solve your "problem." Read it through once, and then go through it again and make notes for yourself.

1. Identify the "problem" in your life.

    a. Would finding a partner really be your solution? If so, who thinks you need a partner?

___Your parents?

___Your friends?

___Society as a whole?

___You?

b. Do the men you meet intensify your "problem?"

___Would meeting a different kind of man solve it?

___Do you keep repeating patterns?

___If so, is there something you gain from being part of these dramas?

c. Would the problem go away if you changed your physical appearance?

___If so, why do you believe this is true?

___What do you get out of looking the way you do?

2. Why has not being married become your "problem"?

    a. Is it the way your parents raised you?

    b. Can it be credited to socio-political forces larger than yourself?

    c. Have personal economics and your profession/career status made being single a "problem"?

    d. Has our quick-fix culture made the quest for a partner frustrating?

    e. Has your search become a never-attainable/perfectionist goal?

___Is there something in you that fears succeeding? That enjoys the drama of complaining?

3. Is the "problem" something you can personally solve or get help solving?

    a. What are the actual causes, not the imagined or frantic ones?

    b. What solutions can work?

    c. What do you do to hold yourself back?

    ___Do you repeat patterns that you can get help in identifying?

    ___Can you restructure your life so that you'll stop repeating them?

4. How do you avert the pain of loneliness?

    a. Make yourself extraordinary?

    b. Create a non-stop work schedule?

    c. Play the numbers dating game?

    ___What might happen if you just let yourself feel lonely?

PRACTICAL CHANGES YOU CAN MAKE:

1. Pick different kinds of partners.

    a. Why is picking different kinds of partners hard?

    b. What are the functions the "wrong" partners fill?

    ___You can stay "free."

    ___You can keep working over unmet emotional needs.

    c. Decide that it's time to give yourself a head start.

____Address your fears of intimacy and tandem fears of abandonment.

____Face your pattern head on. Create some basic ground rules. (e.g., Don't date anyone who is not immediately open and available for a primary romantic relationship.)

2. Adjust your expectations for relationships.

    a. Make a cost–benefit analysis of a committed relationship.

    ____Why do you want a committed relationship?

    ____Why might you not want a committed relationship?

    b. Is monogamy important? Why?/Why not?

    ____Has monogamy been your personal choice or has it been a cultural overlay that you've blindly accepted?

    ____Would there be benefits to a non–monogamous relationship?

    c. Is having children with a partner important?

    ____What would be the benefits/losses of having a baby on your own?

    ____Do you have time to wait for your partner to be ready to parent a child with you? Is the time frame realistic for you?

    ____Do you treat the people you date more as potential co-parents than as potential life partners? Does this keep you from creating the relationship you really want?

    d. Do you get involved with men you don't really respect?

    ____What needs do these involvements meet for you?

    ____Do these involvements ultimately create frustration?

_____What do you fear losing if you were to involve yourself with someone you did respect?

3. See the social context of your "problem."

    a. See how you are not alone in these fears and that your experiences are probably not unique.

    b. Make a realistic assessment of what kinds of personal changes are possible.

EMOTIONAL MAPS AND HOW TO REPAIR THEM

We all have emotional maps. These are the cultural and class-based guidelines our parents gave us for navigating the world. Many professional people today were raised using emotional maps that couldn't possibly help them in adulthood. There may be a huge disparity between their worlds then and now. Perhaps they've since immigrated to a new country or culture or received education and career opportunities that no one prepared them for socially and emotionally.

Susan, whom we discussed in Chapter One, had a working-class emotional map that caused her much difficulty as a professional adult. A college professor, she is fraught with nagging insecurities that she'll be "exposed" as a fake:

> I'm always fearing that I'll get caught—that the school and my students will find out I'm a fraud, that I don't know very much—that I'm not very good. I continue to emotionally dismiss the high ratings my students give me, believing that they're just telling me these things to get an "A," and that I'm really not very good and will soon get caught by "the boss" and get fired.

Occasionally, Susan even sabotages herself to confirm her own self-image. Her insecurities make it hard for her to relate to people who don't have them. When she meets a confident person, she feels like "cowering in the cracks—it's too scary for me to admit to them how insecure I feel."

Susan reflects her childhood emotional map of not having enough and thus not deserving much in her involvement with unavailable men:

Although I've lost interest in sweets, which were the good things in childhood (I put tremendous effort into sneaking cakes, cookies and nuts that my Mom hid—I'd take just enough so that she wouldn't immediately notice anything was missing), today sex is pretty much that desired but scarce commodity. It's emotionally uninteresting to me to be with someone who wants to get together all the time. What's interesting is someone who lives out of town, is married, or otherwise involved. Then I can dream about how perfect they are and see them so infrequently that I couldn't possibly get smothered, trapped, or lost. It's gotten to the point where I don't even get attracted to openly available men.

If you, like Susan, have an emotional map that brings you more grief than happiness, you can begin to repair it by doing the following:

1. Locate troublesome behavior (e.g., fear of entrapment, fear of abandonment, need for approval, fear of intimacy, excessive thriftiness).

2. Examine the values you were taught. Whose were they? Under what conditions were they effective?

3. Describe your emotional map.

4. Describe the world you now live in with particular regard to the (ineffective) emotional map you've been applying.

5. Assess the net effect of applying this emotional map (e.g., success inhibited, relationships stunted, social isolation).

6. Release yourself from your emotional map. Accept that it is not useful for who you are and all who you want to become.

7. See how your fears are linked to the contradictions you've been living. Give yourself time to do things well. Let the fears come up—talk them out. Meditate.

8. Devise an emotional map that is functional for who you've become.

9. Devise values that work for you now.

10. Make these values yours. (It can be difficult to reconcile deep emo-

tions with today's reality.)

11. Make authenticity checks. Realize that there will be moments when your new map and new values won't yet feel right.

12. Make peace with your old values. Allow yourself release time to act out the patterns of your old map—you may only be able to rid yourself of them when you can face head-on the pain they bring.

Talk To Your Dark Side And Make It Your Friend

We all have dark sides rife with bitterness, obsessiveness, and accusation. We live in a culture that tells us to cover it up and wear a happy face. Women especially are not supposed to show anger, disappointment, and frustration.

In our culture we largely numb our dark sides through non-stop activity and substance addiction. Rather than averting the pain of loneliness and other dark feelings, look them straight in the eye. Have a conversation with them. Give them a name. Find out how old they are and what makes them come out. Listen to their pain. Listen to their worries. Give them a voice. Show them respect. Stop numbing them out and blurring them away. The more respect you show them, the less they'll need to cry and scream in pain.

Rona, thirty-six, a veteran of numerous love, intimacy, and relationship workshops, finds that she has to go inside herself rather than blurring out her obsessions by running around and complaining:

I've come to realize that I can't be run by that obsessive voice that wants to be loved. I have to love myself. The way I began loving myself was to talk to that voice. I gave her a name. We began having conversations. I listened to her fear of abandonment—I listened to the part of her that doesn't feel whole unless some man is validating her femininity by calling her. I held her and let her cry.

How I Began To Make Peace With My Parents

When I told my parents I was a woman who *may* never marry, they were not particularly pleased. Filled with thoughts of sexless, lonely spinsters, they worried that on my own, I might be deficient or unhappy.

For years, my mother would fret over my lack of security, which to her was demonstrated by my not having health insurance. She contended that if I were to marry, I could get on my husband's plan and then she wouldn't have to worry about my well-being. I proposed a counter-argument that quieted her: First, not every man who could marry me has a health insurance plan I might want to join; besides, if I want health insurance, I can buy my own it if that is how I choose to spend my money.

What I really heard her saying was, "I'm scared that no one cares for you the way your dad has cared for me." First, I affirmed that my dad's caring for her was indeed wonderful, though truthfully she was one man away from poverty. Second, I explained that in terms of caring and emotional support, she was all wrong. I offered the comparison of my life in my thirties to hers. When she was in her thirties, she lived in a house in the suburbs and spent all day caring for two youngsters. Her only adult conversations were held with my father when he wasn't at work. There were no other men in her life. In contrast, my life in my thirties has been immensely rich and varied. I have at least ten men in my life with whom I share personal matters, plus another twenty-five with whom I've been close over the last fifteen years. Some of these men have collaborated with me on creative projects, some have been lovers, others colleagues, co-workers and housemates . . . all have been immensely important to my life. I also happen to have a man who is my primary love interest; while I enjoy his company, I don't need from him all the things that she needed from Dad.

Eventually, Mom conceded I had a real point. She then expressed regret that she hadn't been able to have real friendships with men. When she and a boyfriend broke up, she'd tear up his picture, return his gifts, and never talk to him again.

My dad has had his own set of anxieties about my non-married condition. These often get expressed in offhand remarks and slightly humorous jokes. He'll say, "That'll be the day when you can take us out for a $100 dinner" . . . or "That'll be the day when you actually make money on your writing" . . . or "when we see one of your shows on prime-time television" . . . "or when you live in a house that has a real guest room."

I then asked if it was really true that he wasn't happy with me. He was a little uneasy when I pointed out that his jokes seemed to have an anxious edge. I then admitted that while it is certainly true that I haven't yet achieved all that I want to, nor all that he wants me to, that's just how things are. I then proposed that since he's in his late eighties, he might not be around to see me achieve all that I do, let alone everything he wants me to. I proposed a playful and perhaps perfect solution. Together we would create a congratulations videotape where he could wish me well on every achievement he'd like for me, regardless of whether it would ever happen (or I even wanted it to happen). The tape might say, "Congratulations on marrying that wonderful guy" . . . "Congratulations on your new home in Malibu" . . . "Congratulations on the birth of your second child" . . . "Congratulations on your tenth best seller."

How I Made Peace With Myself

For years I felt inadequate that I hadn't earned much money, owned much materially, or had children. As I began to research this book, my perspective on myself drastically shifted. I interviewed plenty of people who have harnessed their earning power and own plenty of stuff, and yet have no sense of who they are. I met people whose children give them no time for themselves, and others who have time for themselves but not a clue as to how to enjoy it.

I began to understand that I was really addressing quality of life issues. To live a satisfying life, we need love, community, comfort, money, self-acceptance, and intimacy. When I compared myself and my life to people who embodied the financial or parental status I had not yet achieved, I realized that I was doing just fine. I admitted that my community and my self-understanding were serving me well, and that my life altogether had few holes that couldn't easily be repaired.

I could feel good because my attitude changed. I truly love the person I have become, the choices I have made, the friendships I have nurtured, and the community I have built. The people around me know this. What is perhaps most satisfying is that it's been a long time since any of my friends have asked me why I'm not married!

Last January, I observed my fortieth birthday with a party that was a true celebration of self. Despite thunderstorms and scarce parking, over 100 friends bearing wonderful gifts came to view an exhibit of my life. Filling every wall of the vacant apartment next door, the exhibit spanned my last forty years of achievements, dramas, traumas, and contemplations. It included things I was proud of, things I was embarrassed about, things many people might consider too private to disclose—things that revealed everything I could about who I am. Preparing the exhibit took weeks of sorting through baby pictures, grade school certificates, high school papers, travel journals, wish lists, TV and film proposals, letters to and from friends, personal journals, press clips, acceptance letters, rejection letters, statements of purpose, paintings, and academic achievements. Though I ended up using perhaps a quarter of what I wanted to, the process of looking over physical evidence of where I came from and what happened along the way was very fulfilling. I accepted all of me—the strange, the quirky, the wonderful, and the creative—as well as my inner beauty and brilliance. Preparing the exhibit and inviting my community of friends to view it helped me truly make peace with myself.

In the next and final chapter, we'll consider external structural changes. Now that you know who you are and why you've been living as you do, you're invited to contemplate ways to build intimacy, community, and create the family life that's right for you.

$\mathscr{F}$AMILIES OF THE $\mathscr{F}$UTURE: $\mathcal{T}$HE $\mathcal{Q}$UEST FOR $\mathcal{I}$NTIMACY AND $\mathcal{C}$OMMUNITY

❖❖

O nce you've made peace with who you are and have perhaps examined the factors and forces that have shaped you
thus far, I invite you to consider how you'd really like to
live. Rather than averting loneliness by patching together a "make-do"
life, imagine what mix of intimacy, family, and community would bring
you the most satisfaction.

Today, a family may be defined in many ways. There are single-
parent families (eleven percent), domestic partnerships (gay and straight,
seven percent), related adults (five and a half percent) dual-income married couples (forty and one-half percent) and single-person households
(twenty-three percent). If you are living on your own, you are in fact
living in one of the more popular family forms!

There's no reason to feel you're missing out if your life does not fit
into the traditional family mold. Even though the traditional Ozzie-and-
Harriet family of the '50s was an aberration for America, it is deeply
embedded in our nation's consciousness. Many of our leaders were parents during that period, while people now in their thirties and forties
grew up in those families. For much of America this period is emotionally imprinted as normal, and they may feel a sense of loss for not
reproducing it.

As an anthropologist, I know that humans have a long tradition of
living in groups. We all came out of bands, tribes, villages and extended

families. If we step back to the generation of our grandparents, the extended family was the ideal, with grandparents, parents, aunts, uncles and children, living nearby, if not all under one roof. That ideal broke down as corporate America offered incentives to young families who would relocate, making the nuclear family the desired family unit. Today, we are witnessing an equally profound shift, with the displacement of family culture by the culture of individual achievement. Here, we measure happiness by material goods rather than by love. We matter when we are able to purchase (and then display) "emblems of achievement" like successful businesses, fancy cars, mansions, stylish clothes, and plastic surgery. Men, especially, may feel safer operating under the edict of the culture of individual achievement because their work then leads to a measurable reward.

THE STATE OF FAMILY IN AMERICA TODAY

Today we are confounded by the near-impossibility of piecing together viable family lives without acknowledging the following myths:

1. That humans mate for life.

2. That men marry as a mark of maturity and are able to effectively support women and children.

3. That the nuclear family is the most effective and viable way to raise children.

4. That women will tolerate anything to keep "the family" intact.

All humans need what families give—social and emotional support, physical touching, and sexual expression. We all need to feel important, to be wanted and to belong. But many of us are not meeting these needs. Rather than trying to cram the more than seventy-seven million single adults, ten million single mothers, as well as gay families, blended families, and "boomerang" families (adult children who boomerang back to live with their parents) into "manageable" nuclear families, we need to face who we are and respond accordingly.

TV character Murphy Brown's choice to have a baby on her own is emblematic of the shift away from nuclear family culture. Most women who choose to give birth do so because they feel confident they can provide a good nest. Their model for family life isn't always the traditional nuclear family, which may not be possible or even desirable.

U.C. Berkeley sociologist Arlie Hochschild contends our fifty percent divorce rate is sure testament to one of the primary reasons women leave men—lack of cooperation with the second shift: housework and child care. But with seventy percent of women working full time (including sixty percent of mothers with infants under one year of age), we need more than fathers to pick up the slack.

We need affordable and safe child care at job sites, neighborhood homes, community centers, school yards, libraries—all day, every day. Care should be available for sick children and for children whose parents work night shifts and swing shifts.

We must also face that single mothers need more income. Rather than chastise them for not conforming to an archaic social order, we should provision them so that their children will be able to fully reap their human potentials. Men have higher wages than women because at the turn of the last century their earnings were marked as the "family-wage" (so that they'd be able to support their families) while women's were considered "pin-money." Today's single mothers are certainly as deserving of family-wage-adjusted salaries as the fathers of yesteryear.

Combining love and marriage is actually a cultural construction. Humans have not always lived this way. During the 11th century, the notion of courtly love meant poetry and songs directed to lovers outside and apart from one's marriage. By the 14th century, the church proclaimed that love and marriage should be linked together. This arrangement worked out fairly well for the next 400 years, since married couples were socially, economically and morally tied to their extended families. Thus women and men didn't have to be everything for each other, as many married couples attempt to do today.

Finally, we need to accept that humans are not particularly monogamous. Nearly seventy percent of married men have affairs, followed closely by fifty-seven percent of married women. Perhaps sociobiologically, through natural selection, we've been programmed to be non-monogamous to insure species survival. The more diversity there is in a gene pool, the greater likelihood there is for a species to survive. The more each male spreads his genes to fertile females, the more likely larger numbers of healthy progeny will be born. And likewise the larger the number of sources a female has for sperm, the greater her chances of producing healthy offspring. Finally, a female who draws from a greater number of males to father her newborn, insures a larger circle of provider/protector fathers. While religious and state ethics may try to stuff our romantic desires into lifelong marriage, many of us are not succeeding. The most typical marital form here in the United States is probably serial monogamy. Rather than battling our wills and/or sneaking around and feeling shameful, we ought to openly embrace our sexual natures. While there's a new wave of self-help books out on how to keep marital life hot and sexy, the truth is that our popular culture promotes falling in love with someone new.

Contrary to the new right's ideas of what our social order should be, we will be seeing fewer Mom-and-Pop households, and more Murphy Brown households. We're now living a realistic adaptation to today's social and economic geography. The traditional nuclear family is now a cultural artifact. Rather than hang onto a dying family form, we need to socially and politically embrace and financially support the many ways we raise children and nurture ourselves.

A Personal Reflection On The Meaning Of And Future For Family

For me the extended family has been primarily a theoretical construct. Extended families were the rule in the U.S. up until the industrial revolution and for at least the first generation of most immigrant families. For the kids in Mani, the Mayan Yucatec village where I began doing field work in the mid-'70s, it is the only reality they know. They grew up down the street from their cousins and saw their grandparents every day. Their biggest fears of leaving town are that they would be living among people who don't know them and whom they couldn't trust.

I reflected on similar fears I might have faced growing up. I readily accepted going away to college—it didn't hit me that I was going to lose ninety-nine percent of my high school friends. Initially they called, wrote and visited on weekends and during breaks. It wasn't until one of my best high school friends got married at twenty-three that I realized my social world had changed for good. Somehow I thought that when we returned from college, we'd be take up our old lives again. She married a corporate financier, they bought a house in a classy Connecticut suburb, and during the five years I lived in New York, she never managed to come down for the weekend. I had a couple of long cries about losing her, and then I just got numb to losing close friends.

Love, jobs and adventures kept tossing whatever connections I managed to forge into the winds of the '60s and '70s. I'd travel and meet great people and just let them be. To survive, I learned not to be possessive, not let anyone matter too much. I learned to have what might best be called "controlled obsessions." I'd have intense crushes, but as soon as they started falling apart, I'd quickly talk myself out of it, pick up the pieces, and move on. Eventually, I learned how to have "segmented relationships"—sex from one person, joking, career support, intellectual stimulation, and emotional sharing from others. This way I'd never appear too needy and could also ensure that no one could know me or control me too well.

Back to Mani. When I'm in Mani, I'm not concerned about being controlled or scared of anyone getting under my skin. Even when people relate unique and weird things they've noticed about me, I still feel safe and accepted. Recently, they admitted that the first time I lived there they thought my contact lenses were really strange. To them it was weird (and perhaps disgusting) to watch me pop these little plastic things out of my eyes and then watch me squint afterwards. Despite their experiencing me as being from another planet, I still felt totally accepted. The most intrusive thing anyone ever did to me there was ask me what I was doing or where I was going. When I answered simply that I was taking a walk or writing things down, this sufficed as completely adequate.

Now, the frightening stuff. If we were to look at the interdependent extended family life in Mani as "normal," then would our urban disintegration of "family" be an indicator of social and moral deterioration? Should we look at the growing numbers of single parents, a divorce rate that hovers at fifty percent, and the unprecedented numbers of people who live alone as indicators of our inability to tolerate physical and social intimacy? Do we assume that our obsessions (like sex and food addictions and substance abuse) are in fact indicative of a culture that is deeply out of alignment because we're deprived of intimacy?

PLURAL MARRIAGE

Let's say you're not interested in replicating the nuclear family, but you do want a loving intimate family life. You might consider creating or joining a group/plural marriage. In most parts of the world, economics is a major factor in choosing polygamy. The polygynous (one male and at least two females) option is frequently exercised by wealthy men. These men may support several wives, either in the same compound or in separate dwellings. A man might take a second wife because his first wife is infertile. Rather than abandoning her, he adds a fertile woman to his household. The Turkana of Kenya (as discussed in Chapter One) routinely marry widowed women into already existent households so that they and their children will be comfortably provided for. Polyandry (one female and more than one male) is practiced in Tibet, where brothers from the same family marry a single wife so they won't have to subdivide their family's farm.

Polygamy, a new form for this culture (though an old one in Africa and among the Mormons), presents many psycho-emotional issues. These include jealousy, possessiveness, the need to feel special, valued, and secure. Most literature and film addresses polygamy negatively. We see co-wives plotting against each other (*Raise the Red Lantern*) and jilted lovers obsessing over killing their replacements (*Lovers*). Nonetheless, with our intense need for independence and freedom, along with our collective desire to belong, plural marriage may be a powerful possibility for the 21st century. Plural marriages could provide more freedom, affection, and accountability. It's possible that spousal abuse would diminish, home-based child care would increase, less smothering and controlling behavior would occur, and spousal communication would improve.

Here in the U.S., a fledgling group of people, some inspired by the communes of the '60s, others by self-styled gurus, and still others by science-fiction paradises, live in (or aspire to live in) some version of a group marriage. (For more information, including a directory of resources, see *Love Without Limits* by Deborah Anapol, $18 from Intinet, Box 4322-U, San Rafael, CA 94913-4322.) Typically, guru-inspired and -controlled group marriages limit rather than expand personal freedom. When there are more people, making decisions is more difficult and conformity is more demanding. The solution, either surrendering to an omnipotent leader or participating in constant consensus building, make such lifestyles challenging.

Perhaps the most notorious for its restrictive rules and unique sexual practices was the San Francisco-based utopian Kerista tribe. Kerista, which fell apart in November 1991, lasted for twenty-five years and involved thirty-five core people. Members were on a rotating sleeping schedule and assigned a different lover for each night of the week. Everyone was expected to have sex every night for the good of the group. Anyone who didn't was shunned. While sex was compulsory, romantic attachments were forbidden. At one time the group's leader banned kissing and fondling because he feared they might create pair bonds that could weaken the group's unity.

Kerista was also an economic family. They pioneered in desktop publishing, bringing their founder considerable wealth. The core members, having joined in their late teens and early twenties, had little or no experience working on their own and were terrified of leaving. Now thrust into mainstream society, they bear a difficult mix of the inexperience of adolescents with the quest for power of adults. They have little experience in attracting and building romantic love bonds and little confidence in working on their own. While for years they had believed they were blazing the utopian community for the 21st century, as splintered individuals, much of their growth has been stunted.

It's certainly not necessary to join a Kerista–style utopian commune to be part of a group marriage. The most basic group marriage unit is a triad. Triads, by design, typically add a single person to an already established couple. Since there is no real precedence for triads in our society, they vary considerably. They can, however, be a durable marital form, with some now lasting well over ten years. Legally, however, they are not yet sanctioned, requiring individual legal agreements to be drawn among the participating parties.

Triads can be heterosexual, homosexual, bisexual or asexual. I've even heard of a triad in which the three partners were economically, socially, and emotionally linked, but express themselves sexually outside of their marriage. Some hetero triads' two women (or two men) alternate nights with the one man (or one woman). Other triads all share the same bed each night. Under these arrangements, the two women, if they are bisexual, are sexual with each other as well as their husband. And it's certainly possible for a heterosexual triad to share the same bed without any homosexual activity.

Triads can be polyfidelitous, meaning they have sex only with each other, or they can be open to each member having additional lovers. Triads are not necessarily three-way love affairs. When a third person is added to an already stable couple, love between all three may not be equal. The initial couple's love may have a different quality and depth than either of them have with the new woman or man. The new person may add lots of excitement to the established couple's relationship. Eventually, though, the new person might feel like the odd man out—

that already established family traditions are too deeply ingrained to fully include him or her.

Creating a triad can also function as a transition from one dyadic relationship to another. Some ten years ago, Vince and Sarah added Rose to their longstanding marriage. Rose and Vince are now deeply in love with each other, while the passion between Vince and Sarah is not as strong. Sarah, while approving of Vince and Rose's relationship, now feels like the third wheel. If Sarah were to find someone who loves her the way Rose and Vince now love each other, she might be perfectly content to go off with him.

Being in a triad usually involves more relationship work than being in a couple. There are more points of view, more feelings and altogether more juice. Unsaid things usually don't stay unsaid as long. There are more people who care. For people who really like all of the tussles and joys of a relationship, triads can expand these manyfold.

EXTENDED FAMILIES OF CHOICE

Extended Families of Choice may very well be the emergent family model. While first-generation immigrants (like many of our grandparents) relied on the extended family for nurture, food, housing, financial assistance, and emotional support, these needs are being filled more frequently and more joyously by our families of choice. A family of choice might include close friends, former lovers/spouses, co-workers, current and former housemates, and romantic partners. Rather than trying to get everything from one other person or trying to find and then force one other person to meet all of our familial needs, we might be better off to expand our family base. Today's eclectic families of choice may very much become our culture's families of the future.

Los Angeles sexologist Helen Vaughn has, over the last twenty-five years, built a functional and loving social, emotional, and sexual extended family. While she lives with her husband, she and he are deeply involved in a network of people who have committed to loving each other for the rest of their lives. When she was hospitalized, Helen arranged for an attractive widowed woman friend to stay with her husband. She explains, "I wanted him to be cared for and comfortable . . . there was no reason he should be home alone."

Vaughn's daughter and her best friend gave birth the same year and often breastfed each other's infants. As their children have grown older, they have taken turns picking them up from day care—they are like one family. When members of the network become widowed, they move in with (and often marry) other survivors. They are truly there for each other for life.

Cohousing, where a group of families and/or individuals purchase, design, and develop land or property so that each household has a separate unit but shares in group facilities originated in Denmark in the early seventies. Over the last several years this concept has captured the imaginations of communal-minded professionals throughout the U.S. (For information about joining or creating a cohousing community see: Cohousing Compendium [Center for Cooperatives, U.C. Davis, 1993] or subscribe to the Cohousing Newsletter; P.O. Box 2584 Berkeley, CA 94702, [510] 528-2212 [$20/year]. Or contact the Cohousing Co.; 1250 Addison St. #113; Berkeley, CA 94702, [510] 549-9980.) Their live-in communities have featured group meals, on-site day-care centers, organic gardens, social halls, Jacuzzis, and a deep interest in living together. Unlike the anonymity found in many apartment and condo complexes, cohousing communities, initiated by people who want to live together, are very social places. And unlike guru-controlled group marriages, there is no prescribed set of social or sexual practices.

Visiting cohousing communities in Emeryville and Davis, Calif., as well as on Bainbridge Island, across the lake from Seattle, Wash., I was impressed. I liked how they allowed single people, as well as otherwise-isolated nuclear families, to be full members of vital extended families. I loved how the children freely play on the communal grounds and are welcomed in each other's homes. That very much reminded me of how the people of Mani raise their children. I liked how members make up for missing and yet-to-be-filled familial needs. In one community, when a husband was left by his wife, he didn't suffer the way a man might have if he lived alone in a single-family house. He could eat with others at the central dining room, had plenty of neighbors with whom he could confide, and remained a full member of his cohousing family.

What did perturb me was the monumental amount of time required for building these communities. Every decision required a group consensus, and at times these groups met as often as three times a week. It was a huge commitment just to have neighbors with a shared communal spirit. I concluded that a day-to-day, face-to-face community life ought to be accessible to all of us whether or not we're interested in or motivated to live in cohousing.

How To Build Your Own Community

If you've been spending perhaps too much of your time trying to meet a Mr. Right, rather than affirming and building your real-life community, consider doing some (or all) of the following:

1. Throw parties and/or get yourself invited to parties, gatherings, and events.
2. Find or organize a weekly salon. These salons can be casual gatherings where artists and thinkers drop by to chat, drink soup, break bread, and share their creations and ideas.

3. Write notes to friends you don't see often.

4. Go through your phone book every couple of months and call people you haven't heard from.

5. Talk on the phone with at least a couple of friends every day.

6. Develop a set of friends you talk to at least every week.

7. Make sure that at least half the people you go out with are not lovers or potential lovers.

Several years ago I moved into a one-bedroom apartment. It was the first time in my life I had ever lived alone. Before then I had always shared my living space with roommates and lovers. That aloneness gave me the impetus to build my own community.

The key things I learned were to create fillable needs and to treat still-casual friends like family. People love satisfying finite manageable requests. Some of the requests I made were for rides to pick up my car from the mechanic, borrowing small or returnable quantities of food, and feeding my cat when I went out of town. These weren't, of course do-or-die needs. And if no one could help me, I'd certainly manage. The point of making these requests was to begin creating a relationship.

As people happily met these needs, I increased them. I asked a woman I was just getting to know if she'd be willing to pick me up at the airport. Rather than telling me to take the super shuttle (as I feared she might), she agreed and thanked me for thinking of her as someone I felt that close to. She admitted that she'd only ask a lover or family member to do such a chore, I nodded and suggested that perhaps we could think of each other as family. After that we regularly took each other to the airport—and had wonderful conversations going and coming. After a while we invited each other for hikes, to parties, and to see movies and plays. I knew we wouldn't have gotten close so quickly if I hadn't created a fillable, familial need.

In a culture where everyone appears to be super-busy and over-extended, loneliness is a very hard thing to admit. Initially, I was reluctant to ask for invitations to parties and gatherings; I hoped that I would be seen as a likable person that people would naturally invite. I found (at least in L.A.) it didn't work that way. I had to let it be known to party-givers and their friends that I wanted to be invited. After a while, I located several key networkers who would call me with invitations and leads. From attending these parties, events, gatherings, and groups, I began to expand my social circle. Gradually, I drew in friends who became so close that I began to regard them as my extended family of choice. Eventually, they would call to discuss the leads for the coming week, and together we would evaluate what might happen and where we might meet up. Then the following week we'd gossip about all the things that had happened that one of us missed. (We didn't need to watch soap operas or read romance novels because we were generating enough on our own!)

One of the last strongholds we have for our blood families is holiday celebrations. While we may tell our real secrets to friends, it's our blood families we see for the holidays. After spending a much too quiet Thanksgiving, I decided to make every effort I could to have a more social Christmas and Chanukah. I announced to the people in my "family" that I wanted to be invited to everything possible. The weekend before Christmas, I went to about five Chanukah/Christmas parties. The following week, I did something fun just about every night, and then on Christmas Eve, I exchanged gifts with friends, sang carols and gave stuffed animals to sick children at a local hospital, and then joined in a new girlfriend's family celebration. There were people of all sizes and shapes and colors . . . and they were fun. I was included in the family pictures and ate lots of delectable food. I had actually loosened up enough to enjoy whatever came my way. My "dream family" was in fact all around me.

There is certainly no one right way to live, love, be loved, or meet your need for family. Whether or not you marry or even have an interest in doing so, you have deep human needs to be intimate and to belong. Once you accept who you are and how you got there, you can begin to explore the possibilities.

You have the freedom to consider a multitude of opportunities. You *may* savor the freedom of living on your own and having a baby on your own as well. You *may* love another woman, have part-time lovers, openly (or secretly) share your lover with others, create your own version of an extended family, and of course you *may* marry a man. Never say never. . . . Savor all the possibilities, and remember there are opportunities for deep satisfaction that lie well beyond the traditional nuclear family.

Works Cited

Chapter One:

Jesse Bernard, *The Future of Marriage*, New York: World, 1972.

Family Diversity in America: Household Characteristics and Demographics by Family Diversity: A Project of Spectrum Institute, P.O. Box 65765; Los Angeles, CA 90065.

Helen Fisher, *Anatomy of Love: The Natural History of Monogamy, Adultery, and Divorce*, New York: Norton, 1992.

"Single Black Women" a report for ABC Television's "20/20," by Karen C. Saunders, April 1991.

"The Marriage Crunch: If You're a Single Woman, Here Are Your Chances of Getting Married," *Newsweek*, June 2, 1986, p. 54-7, 61. Interestingly, Neil Bennett, David Bloom and Patricia Craig, the authors of the research paper that fueled the headlines, omitted their controversial findings when they officially published their research in the *American Journal of Sociology* 95, 3 in November 1989 p. 692-722.

Thomas Exter, in "How to Figure Your Chances of Getting Married," *American Demographics*, June 1987, p. 50-52.

Barbara Ehrenreich, Elizabeth Hess and Gloria Jacobs, *Remaking Love: The Feminization of Sex*, Garden City, New York: Anchor Press/ Doubleday, 1987.

Susan Faludi, *BACKLASH: The Undeclared War Against American Women*, New York: Crown, 1991.

Chapter Two:
Marjorie Shostak, *NISA: The Life and Words of a !Kung Woman*, New York: Vintage Books, 1981.

Steven Mintz and Susan Kellog, *Domestic Relations: A Social History of American Family Life*, New York: Macmillan Free Press, 1988, p. 57-58.

Ellen K. Rothman, *Hearts and Hands: A History of Courtship in America*, Cambridge: Harvard University Press, 1987, p. 252.

Laura Doan, *Old Maids to Radical Spinsters: Unmarried Women in the Twentieth-Century Novel*, Chicago: University of Illinois Press, 1991, pg. 6-8.

Reay Tannahill, *Sex in History*, New York: Stein and Day, 1980, p. 338-373.

John D'Emilio and Estelle B. Freedman, *Intimate Matters: A History of Sexuality in America*, New York: Harper and Row, 1988, p. 132-135.

Gail Warshofsky Lapidus, *Women in Soviet Society: Equality, Development, and Social Change*, Berkeley: University of California Press, 1978, p. 257-258.

Bernice Madison, "Social Services for Women: Problems and Priorities," In *Women in Russia* edited by Dorothy Atkinson, Alexander Dallin, and Gail Warshofsky Lapidus. Palo Alto: Stanford University Press, 1977, p. 308-309.

Karen Kelsey, "Sex and the Gaijin Male: Contending Discourses on Race and Gender in Contemporary Japan." Paper delivered to the American Anthropological Association 1992 Meeting, San Francisco, CA.

Barbara Levy Simon, *Never Married Women*, Temple University Press, 1987, p. 94-110.

Chapter Three:
Gloria Steinem, *Revolution from Within: A Book of Self-Esteem*, Boston: Little, Brown and Company, 1992, p. 256.

Ellen Kreidman, *Light His Fire: How to Keep Your Man Passionately and Hopelessly in Love with You*, New York: Villard Books, 1989.

Chapter Five:
"Gone Today, Hair Tomorrow? The Commercialization and Medicalization of Natural Hair Loss Among Healthy American Males," paper delivered by Kenyon Stebbins to the American Anthropological Association, November 28, 1990, New Orleans, LA.

Margaret Kent, *How to Marry the Man of Your Choice*, New York: Warner, 1988.

Tracy Cabot, *How to Make a Man Fall in Love With You*, New York: St. Martin's, 1985.

Sonya Friedman, *Men Are Just Desserts*, New York: Warner Books, 1983.

Colette Dowling, *The Cinderella Complex*, New York: Pocket Books, 1981.

Penelope Russianoff, *Why Am I Nothing Without a Man?* New York: Bantam Books, 1984.

Connell Cowan and Melvyn Kinder, *Smart Women: Foolish Choices*, New York: Signet Books, 1985.

Toni Grant, *Being a Woman*, New York: Avon Books, 1988.

Jean Shinoda Bolen, *Goddesses in Everywoman: A New Psychology of Women*, New York: Harper and Row, 1984.

Sally Ogle Davis, "Is Feminism Dead?" *Los Angeles Magazine*, February 1989, p. 118.

Chapter Six:
Warren Farrell, *Why Men Are The Way They Are*, New York: McGraw–Hill, 1986.

Elaine Tyler May, *Great Expectations: Marriage & Divorce in Post-Victorian America*, Chicago: The University of Chicago Press, 1980.

Ehrenreich, Barbara, *The Hearts of Men: American Dreams and the Flight From Commitment*, New York: Anchor Press, 1983.

Everything Men Know About Women, Newport House; 107 R.R. 620 S. Suite 7–A; Austin, TX 78734.

John Gray, *Men Are From Mars, Women Are From Venus*, San Francisco: HarperCollins, 1992.

Debra Tannen, *You Just Don't Understand: Women and Men in Conversation*, New York: Ballantine Books, 1990.

Herb Goldberg, *What Men Really Want*, New York, Signet, 1991.

Gross, Alan, "The Male Role and Heterosexual Behavior" in *Men's Lives* edited by M.S. Kimmel and M.A. Messner, New York: Macmillan, 1988.

Chapter Eight:
Elisabeth Badinter, *The Unopposite Sex: The End of the Gender Battle*, New York: Harper and Row, 1989.

Rose Oldfield Hayes, "Female Genital Mutilation, Fertility Control, Women's Roles, and the Patrilineage in Modern Sudan: A Functional Analysis" in *American Ethnology*, vol. 2, no. 4, pp. 617–631.

Verrier Elwin, *Kingdom of the Young*, Oxford: Oxford University Press, 1968.

Chapter Ten:
Arlie Hochschild, *The Second Shift: Working Parents and the Revolution at Home*, New York: Viking, 1989.

Kathryn McCamant and Charles Durrett, *Cohousing: A Contemporary Approach to Housing Ourselves*, Berkeley: Ten Speed Press, 1988.